101 Great Games for KIDS

Active, Bible-Based Fun for Christian Education

Jolene L. Roehlkepartain

Abingdon Press
Nashville

101 GREAT GAMES FOR KIDS
Active Bible-Based Fun for Christian Education

Copyright © 2000 by Abingdon Press

This book is printed on recycled, acid-free, elemental chlorine–free paper.

Library of Congress Cataloging-in-Publication Data

Roehlkepartain, Jolene L., 1962-
    101 great games for kids : active, Bible-based fun for Christian education / by Jolene L. Roehlkepartain.
        p. cm.
    Includes index.
    ISBN 0-687-08795-3 (alk. paper)
    1. Games in Christian education.   2. Church work with children.   I. Title: One hundred one great games for kids.   II. Title: One hundred and one great games for kids.   III. Title.

BV1536.3 .R64 2000
268'.432—dc21

00-029330

Scripture quotations marked (TEV) are from the Today's English Version—Second Edition, Copyright © 1992 by American Bible Society. Used by permission.

Scripture quotations marked (NIV) are taken from the HOLY BIBLE, NEW INTERNATIONAL VERSION®. NIV®. Copyright © 1973, 1978, 1984 by International Bible Society. Used by permission of Zondervan Publishing House. All rights reserved.

01 02 03 04 05 06 07 08 09—10 9 8 7 6 5 4 3

MANUFACTURED IN THE UNITED STATES OF AMERICA

To Kris Jacobson
for our deep friendship and
for always inspiring me by the way you laugh
and play with children

Contents

Introduction

When people ask me about my favorite part of the Bible, I usually get strange looks after I respond.

"I love the stories in the book of Daniel," I say.

"You mean you like apocalyptic literature?" people sometimes ask. "I suppose Revelation is your second favorite."

No, Revelation doesn't come close to being on my top 10 list. But the stories of Daniel, particularly the story of the fiery furnace in chapter 3, stick with me. And those stories stay with me because of my childhood religious education. Somewhere in my childhood, one of my wise Sunday school teachers taught the story of the fiery furnace by taking our class down to the church basement to the dark, cobweb-filled boiler room. Not only did I hear the story, but I also felt it. I smelled it. I saw it. After that, I had no question what it must have been like to be Shadrach, Meshach, and Abednego, especially since the teacher said the furnace mentioned in the Bible was probably a hundred times hotter than the boiler room and that the guards who threw the three men into the furnace died from the heat. Even today, I shudder when I'm near a church boiler room.

To imprint the story further into my soul, my church did a musical during my fifth-grade year. The musical? About the fiery furnace. Almost thirty years later, I still know the words to "It's Cool in the Furnace" and "Shadrach, Meshach, and Abednego." These Christian education experiences helped me understand Frederick Buechner's interpretation: that "Nebuchadnezzar, King of Babylon, was a real horror."[1]

Even though I was a faithful Sunday school attender, I don't remember most of the lessons that were taught. Instead, I remember the teachers who made me feel special and loved. And I remember the lessons that tapped into all my senses—not just one or two.

The Power of Play

Teaching children well involves understanding them. Four-year-olds are not little adults, and ten-year-olds aren't a closer version.

Children at different ages have different abilities. (See "Children—Age by Age" on pp. 14–15.) Particularly for younger children, playing and learning are one and the same. Young children simply are developmentally incapable of learning without playing.

Even Shinichi Suzuki, the educator who taught three-year-olds how to play the violin, took advantage of this aspect of child development. Suzuki taught three-year-olds by first giving them a violin to play with as a toy. Violin music would be playing as background music during the playtime. Every once in a while, the child would be shown the correct way to play in such a way that the child thought the activity was a game. Gradually, the child learned notes. "This is the art of education," Suzuki writes. "The thing that matters is the result: that the child acquires the skill."[2]

Which skills do we want the children in our churches to acquire? We want children to develop an understanding and appreciation of their religious heritage. We want children to know the scriptures so that the stories within the Bible become their stories. We want children to become lifelong churchgoers who are—and feel like—important members of the faith community. And we want children to develop a faith that has integrity, a faith that stirs them to act in loving, caring, and just ways.

So how do we do that?

Through fun and games.

Unfortunately, our society has labeled "fun and games" as a waste of time, as a way to goof off and not get things done. But when it comes to teaching children in ways that they'll always remember—and in ways that make them want to return to church each week—we have to pull out the fun and games.

That doesn't mean gathering up some balls and board games. It means preparing our lessons and recreation times by using games that teach children about God, faith, and people of the Bible. And that's what this book is all about. It's about teaching children through games.

"You don't just think with your brain," writes author David Gelernter, "you think with your brain and body both."[3] That's true for people of all ages. But for children in particular, you need to get their bodies in motion to get their heads going in that direction. "Movement is essential to learning," writes Carla Hannaford, Ph.D., in *Smart Moves: Why Learning Is Not All in Your Head*. "Movement awakens and activates many of our mental capacities. Movement integrates and anchors new information and experiences."[4]

Of course, you can go overboard. I had a four-year-old once who complained that the thing he hated most about my class was that he got all sweaty. "Can't we just sit down and you read us a story?" he begged. That boy taught me a lot about pacing. Children need movement and games, but they need quiet times, too.

Games for Teaching Well

Unfortunately, few resources exist that feature games that teach important lessons. You'll find books of icebreakers and community builders, and you'll find games that build specific muscles. But rarely will you find a resource that aims to build the whole child: the child's body, mind, social interactions, emotions, and spirit.

That's why when I prepare a Sunday school lesson, I end up using only part of the curriculum. The other part I create. I develop games that get kids moving and emphasize the lesson's point. I create activities that get children to interact with each other so that they develop relationships. I design experiences that get children to talk about their feelings and their experiences. And I create activities that give them hands-on experiences to develop their spirits. By the end of each hour, I can ask each child what was learned, and each will tell me the point of the lesson. That's because they have heard it, felt it, seen it, and sometimes even smelled or tasted it.

When playing games with children, follow a few general principles: Make sure everyone understands the rules. Practice the game once before playing it. Create fair teams. Invite and encourage all children to play. Stop a game while everyone still is having fun instead of waiting until children are tired of the game. Enjoy your playing time together.

Use this book to add life to your educational curriculum. Integrate some of the games into congregational intergenerational events (even adults should move, too). Spice up a church child-care session by sprinkling in a game here and there. Create children's ministry events that get kids excited about the fun—and the learning.

We want to make learning opportunities for children worthwhile so that they keep coming back for more. We want to stir children's imaginations and their passions so that they become interesting and interested people. Learning is, after all, a lifelong process. And learning won't last long if children become bored and restless.

So, instead of getting children to settle down and sit still, have them jump up and move. Engage their bodies. Engage their emotions. And in the process, you'll engage their brains to open up and learn, learn, learn.

Children–Age by Age

For Preschoolers (Ages 3 to 5)

The Mind (Intellectual Development)
- Language bursts from about 750 words (at age 3) to about 5,000 words (at age 5).
- They have a limited attention span.
- They learn mainly through experience and the five senses.
- They're curious and enjoy learning (if that has been and continues to be nurtured by adults).
- They follow one-step directions (at age 3) and three-step directions (at age 5).
- They learn the correct labels for shapes, names, and some colors.
- They have an active imagination and enjoy fantasy play.

The Body (Physical Development)
- They're physically active and need to move and stretch frequently.
- They practice and slowly master specific body skills, such as hopping and skipping.
- They learn self-care, such as dressing, undressing, brushing teeth, and so on.
- They're more apt to move around than to sit still.
- They draw people with two to four body parts by about age four or five.
- They stand on one foot, hop, climb, and kick and throw balls.

The Interactions (Social Development)

- They cooperate with playmates and want to please them.
- Most express anger and frustration with others by getting physical (as by hitting).
- They begin interacting more with children as they age.
- They seek out individual attention.
- They enjoy adults, particularly parents, teachers, and caregivers.
- They're self-centered and assert independence at times.
- They react on a feeling level: clapping and jumping when happy; resisting and arguing when unhappy.

The Emotions (Emotional Development)

- Fears develop as the imagination emerges.
- Some may have imaginary friends.
- They move in and out of fantasy and reality, usually unable to distinguish between the two until age four or five.
- They need adults who take their emotions seriously, even if upset by an imaginary incident.
- They express their emotions through play, such as slaying imaginary dinosaurs and kissing the owies of injured dolls and stuffed animals.
- They act in highly emotional ways but can learn to use words instead of actions.

The Spirit (Spiritual Development)

- They understand God's love through people expressing love toward them rather than hearing about it.
- They enjoy simple, spontaneous prayers.
- They develop a view of God by the way adults treat them.
- Most soak up adults' feelings about God.
- Many desire to participate in meaningful, age-appropriate religious rituals.
- They want to help others as part of helping God.

The Mind (Intellectual Development)
- They learn best through active participation.
- They're focused in the present, not the future.
- They better understand time and time sequence.
- They enjoy hearing about the past, particularly their personal past.
- They're interested in learning about other people and other countries.
- They begin to master reading and writing.
- Most have a strong sense of what's right and wrong.
- They want explanations and often ask "Why?"

The Body (Physical Development)
- They're becoming more coordinated.
- Most are restless at times—wanting to go outside when they're in and wanting to go inside when they're out.
- Many move constantly—even when sitting.
- They enjoy physical, boisterous play.
- Most tend to be full of activity rather than focusing and accomplishing physical tasks.
- They need guidance in recognizing their body signals (fatigue, hunger, and stress).

The Interactions (Social Development)
- They like to please adults.
- Most enjoy playing as part of a group.
- They gradually learn social values, such as honesty, responsibility, and sportsmanship.
- Squabbling and tattling are common for younger ages, and gradually ease with age.
- Most want a personal, separate relationship with adults around them.
- They need guidance from adults to develop socially acceptable behavior.

The Emotions (Emotional Development)

- They tap into their emotions quickly and can still act in highly emotional ways.
- Many have strong likes and dislikes.
- Most enjoy doing things right.
- They gradually develop more of a sense of control over their emotions.
- Sulking, worrying, complaining, and pouting are common.
- They have little interest in self-care and personal grooming.
- They need guidance from adults in articulating their inner feelings.

The Spirit (Spiritual Development)

- Their belief in God is strong, especially if they come from a religious background.
- They enjoy hearing Bible stories.
- Most expect God to answer all their prayers.
- Religious skepticism can appear if they come from families where religion isn't emphasized.
- Some older children may begin to interpret painful events as punishments from God.
- Most tend to believe what others tell them to believe.

For Fourth- to Sixth-Graders (Ages 9 to 12)

The Mind (Intellectual Development)
- Reading skills are more developed, so children "read to learn" rather than "learn to read."
- Many enjoy memorizing facts.
- They still learn best by concrete, hands-on experiences.
- They're more persistent in learning, particularly when they see accomplishment.
- Most like to talk and express their thoughts.
- They're eager to learn more and tackle new challenges.

The Body (Physical Development)
- They enjoy showing their physical skills and strengths.
- They slouch and sit in odd positions.
- Many will push themselves past physical exhaustion unless monitored by adults.
- Growth accelerates in girls, and they become taller and heavier than boys.
- Some can become sedentary, particularly by grade six.
- They enjoy competitive activity.

The Interactions (Social Development)
- They're less self-centered and recognize others' needs and views.
- Most become more interested in friends than family.
- They worship heroes and celebrities.
- They express strong likes and dislikes toward particular people.
- Most cooperate better in groups.
- They have a strong sense of fair play.
- Boys play with boys; girls play with girls.

The Emotions (Emotional Development)
- Most express emotion through subtle movements, such as drumming on a table, holding their breath, or whistling.

- Boys may be more physically and emotionally expressive of anger and frustration; girls may be quieter and giggle and whisper.
- Many growl, sulk, mutter, and blame others when things don't go well.
- They begin to become more self-conscious.
- They're fearful about death and possible family tragedy.
- Many use facial expressions to show emotion.

The Spirit (Spiritual Development)
- Some may find the concept of God as distant from their experience.
- Beliefs begin to taper off, since this age emphasizes rational thought.
- Some may begin to resist going to Sunday school and church.
- They may begin to ask challenging faith questions.
- They need guidance from adults in dealing with their beliefs and their feelings of pain, guilt, struggle, and grief.
- Some may have an unwavering belief in God, particularly if their family has a strong faith.

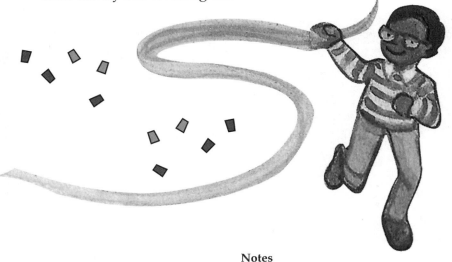

Notes

1. Frederick Buechner, *Peculiar Treasures: A Biblical Who's Who* (San Francisco: Harper & Row, 1979), 117.

2. Shinichi Suzuki, *Nurtured by Love: A New Approach to Education* (New York: Exposition Press, 1969), 108.

3. David Gelernter, *The Muse in the Machine* (New York: Free Press, 1994), 35.

4. Carla Hannaford, Ph.D., *Smart Moves: Why Learning Is Not All in Your Head* (Arlington, Va.: Great Ocean Publishers, 1995), 96.

Section 1

Great Games for PRESCHOOLERS

Games that delight preschoolers tickle their imaginations and invite them to experience the world from a different perspective. Often preschoolers are already in one of these other worlds when they arrive at your setting. Some come dressed as superheroes or fairies, while others may look like nothing is up but begin to purr and meow when you compliment them.

Games for preschoolers not only should stretch their imaginations but also challenge their skills. Children at this age are learning a lot of labels—shapes, colors, animal names, numbers, and letters of the alphabet. They're learning how to hop, climb, kick, and throw balls. When preschoolers learn through play, they find that learning can be fun and enjoyable, which motivates them to learn even more.

The best games for preschoolers are simple. Three-, four-, and five-year-olds do well with games that have one- or two-step directions. They enjoy following instructions and trying new activities. Preschoolers are highly sensory, enjoying games that allow them to move, make sounds, touch, taste, smell, and see. Whenever you can make their world—and the worlds within their imaginations—concrete and real through games, preschoolers will jump in with enthusiasm and play and play and play.

Hezekiah's Gold

Scripture: King Hezekiah needs gold (2 Kings 17–19)

This Game Teaches: When we need something that we don't have, we often can find it when we look.

Materials: Prior to the game, cut several circles out of yellow construction paper and place them around the room, taping them to walls, chairs, the floor, and so forth. Remember to keep track of the total number of yellow circles you placed.

• • • • • • • • • • • • • • • • •

Game: Say: **"King Hezekiah in the Bible had a big problem. There was a bad king who wanted to hurt King Hezekiah and his people. So King Hezekiah told the bad king, 'If you leave, I will give you anything that you want.' Well, the bad king wanted gold. Lots of gold. King Hezekiah didn't have any gold, but he figured out that if everyone pulled the gold from the temple walls, that would be how he could pay the bad king.**

"So, let's do that now. Look around the room. Look for yellow circles of gold. Run around and pull these circles from the walls, floors, etc." When they think they've found them all, count the pieces. If they don't have the total number you hid, send them looking again until all the yellow circles are found.

After the game ends, say: **"King Hezekiah didn't know where he would get the gold at first, but then he remembered the gold in the temple. That's how he was able to pay the bad king. When we need something we don't have, we often can find it when we look."**

Walk, Run, Walk

Scripture: Crossing the Red Sea (Exodus 13:17–14:1-31)
This Game Teaches: God keeps God's people safe.
Materials: None

. . . .

Game: Gather the children around you. Say: **"Moses and God's people were captured by a bunch of bad guys led by a guy named Pharaoh. One day, Pharaoh let Moses and God's people go. Let's pretend we are following God right after Pharaoh freed us. Let's spread out, and I want you to act out what I say to do."** Name the specific instructions listed below one at a time, and do the actions with the children.

- Pharaoh, the bad guy, just freed us. Jump up and down. Cheer!
- Look up in the sky! God is leading the way in a cloud.
- Let's walk and follow God all day.
- Now it's nighttime. Let's put up tents for sleeping.
- Lie down and go to sleep now.
- It's morning. Time to stretch and wake up.
- Look up in the sky! God is still there in the cloud.
- Let's keep walking and following God.
- Oh! Oh! I hear a noise! Who's behind us?
- It's Pharaoh and the bad guys. Quick, let's run!
- Stop! There's a sea in front of us. It's as big as an ocean. How are we going to get across?
- Moses is raising his arms. Look! The sea is parting. We can walk across the sea! Let's walk.
- Oh no! The bad guys are behind us! Hurry to the other side.
- Whew! We made it to the other side.
- But oh, no! Here come the bad guys again! I'm so scared.
- Look! The water is closing! The bad guys are drowning.
- Hooray for God! Hooray for God! We're safe.
- Let's keep walking and following God.

After the game say: **"God still is with us and keeps us safe. God was there for Moses, and God is here for us."**

Come with Me

Scripture: Jesus calls the disciples to follow him (Matthew 4:18-20)

This Game Teaches: Jesus called many to follow him, and we should follow him, too.

Materials: None

. . . .

3

Game: Have the children spread out around the room and sit down on the floor. Ask for a volunteer. Say: **" [child's name] is going to be Jesus and will walk around the room. When Jesus taps your shoulder and says, 'Come with me,' jump up and follow right behind Jesus. Then Jesus will find another person and ask that person to also follow. That person gets at the end of the line. The game ends when everyone is following Jesus. Any questions?"**

Play the game. Afterward say: **"Jesus called many people to follow him. The twelve disciples are known for following Jesus. Even today, Jesus wants people to follow him. We should follow Jesus, too."**

Two! Two! Two!

Scripture: Animals go two by two into the ark (Genesis 7:5-9)
This Game Teaches: No one went into the ark alone.
Everyone got to bring a friend. It's good to have a friend.
Materials: None

● ● ● ● ● ● ● ● ● ● ● ● ● ● ● ● ● ● ●

Game: Have each child find a partner. If an odd number of children are present, play along with the children so that everyone has a partner. Say: **"With your partner, choose an animal that both of you can be. Pick an animal with a sound that you and your partner can make, such as a dog that barks or a horse that whinnies."** Have each pair demonstrate its animal sound to the group.

Then have the partners separate and spread out around the room. Encourage partners to move far away from one another. Say: **"We're going to skip around the room. When I say that it's beginning to rain, start making your animal noise. Run and find your partner and link arms.** (Demonstrate this.) **Then we'll form a line and march into the imaginary ark over there.** (Point to a certain area of the room.) **Any questions?"**

Play the game. After you march into the ark, play the game a couple more times. Then say: **"No one went into the ark alone. Everyone got to bring a friend. Everyone went into the ark two by two. It's good to have a friend."**

4

A Good Helper

Scripture: The good Samaritan (Luke 10:30-37)

This Game Teaches: The Samaritan was a good helper, and
we can be good helpers, too.

Materials: One self-adhesive bandage for each child

• • • • • • • • • • • • • • • • • •

5

Game: Ask for a volunteer to lie on the floor as
if he or she is hurt.
Say: **"We're
going to act out
a story in the
Bible called 'The
Good Samaritan.'
First, we're all
going to act like the
men who wouldn't
help the hurt per-
son. Let's all walk
by our hurt per-
son and not stop
and help."** Do
this with the
children. Then
take them to another
side of the room. Give
each person a bandage.

Say: **"Now we're going to be good helpers. We're going to be
like the good Samaritan. This time when we see the hurt person, we're going to stop and each put a bandage on the person.
Any questions?"** Lead the children to the hurt child. Have everyone put her or his bandage on the child.

After the game ends, say: **"The Samaritan was a good helper,
and we can be good helpers, too. We can help people when
they're hurt. We can help our parents when they need help. We
can all be good helpers."**

Love One Another

Scripture: Love one another as God loves us (1 John 4:7-10)
This Game Teaches: It's good to love one another.
Materials: None

• • • • • • • • • • • • • • • • •

Game: Have children sit in a circle. Say: **"We're going to say 'love one another' in many different ways. Listen close-ly and say 'love one another' in the way that I tell you."**
Use a variety of ways, such as:

- Let's whisper.
- Let's shout.
- Let's sing.
- Let's use our lowest voices.
- Let's use our highest voices.
- Let's say it slowly.
- Let's say it really fast.
- Let's say it a bunch of times.
- Let's say it all together one more time!

After the game say: **"God loves us, and God wants us to love one another. It's good to love God, and it's good to love one another."**

I Know Your Name

Scripture: God knows us even before we are born (Psalm 139:13-15)

This Game Teaches: Each one of us is important to God.

Materials: A beach ball

• • • • • • • • • • • • • • • • • •

7

Game: Have the children sit in a circle with you. Holding the beach ball in your hands, say: **"We're going to play a name game. We're going to take turns rolling the ball across the circle. Before you roll the ball, however, say the name of the person you're rolling it to. Even if the ball rolls to** another person, the person you named should get it. After you get the ball, choose someone else in the circle, say that person's name, and roll the ball to her or him. Any questions?"** Play the game.

Afterward say: **"Our names are so important. They tell who we are. God knows each one of us by name. God even knew us before we were born. Each one of us is important to God."**

Pass the Food!

Scripture: Feeding of the four thousand (Mark 8:1-10)
This Game Teaches: There was enough food for everybody. Jesus took care of people in Bible times, and Jesus takes care of us today.
Materials: Plain doughnuts

• • • • • • • • • • • • • • • • •

Game: Have children stand in a circle. Hold up a doughnut and say: **"Oh no! We're all hungry, but we have only one doughnut. What should we do?"** Invite ideas. Then say, **"I know. Let's share. We'll pass the doughnut around the circle. Tear off as little as you can so that there will be enough for everybody. After you tear off your little bit, eat it."** Start the doughnut around the circle. If you run out before it gets around the circle, start another doughnut in its place. If a large portion of the doughnut remains after everyone has had a little to eat, keep passing the doughnut around until it's gone. After the game ends, say: **"There's a story in the Bible about a time when many, many people** came to hear Jesus talk. It got to be late and everybody was hungry. So the disciples passed around the little food that was there. Everyone got a little bit. There was enough food for everybody, just like everybody got a little bit of the doughnut. Jesus took care of the people then, and Jesus takes care of us today."

8

Tell the Truth!

Scripture: Micah steals silver (Judges 17:1-2)
This Game Teaches: God likes it when we tell the truth.
Materials: A small toy that children can hide in their hands

• • • • • • • • • • • • • • • • •

9

Game: Have the children stand in a circle. Give one child a small toy. Ask for a volunteer to stand in the middle of the circle. Say: **"We're going to play a guessing game. Hold your hands behind your back. Pass the toy around the circle so that the person in the middle can't see who has it. You can pretend to pass the item, or you can really pass it. Try to fool the person in the middle. When I say to stop, everyone stop, and the person in the middle must then guess who has the toy. If he or she is correct, the person with the toy must come into the middle. If he or she is incorrect, we'll keep playing. Any questions?"**

After the game ends, say: **"In the Bible, there's a story about Micah and his mom. Micah stole silver from his mom, and she was wondering who took it. Micah hid it like we hid the toy. But Micah eventually told his mom the truth. God likes it when we tell the truth."**

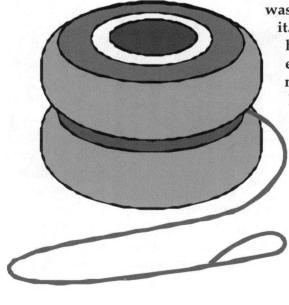

Giggles and Laughter

Scripture: Sarah laughs about the idea of having a baby (Genesis 18:1-15)

This Game Teaches: We sometimes laugh when things are funny or we think something is impossible, but nothing is impossible with God.

Materials: None

• • • • • • • • • • • • • • • • •

Game: Have the children stand in a circle. Say: **"We're going to go around the circle and take turns laughing. I'll go first. Then we will go this way** (show the direction) **around the circle."** Begin the game. After everyone has had a chance to laugh, ask the children to follow these commands:

* Everyone laugh soft.
* Everyone laugh loud.
* No one laugh. (Do this when children have the giggles and may have a hard time stopping.)
* Laugh around the circle again.

After the game say: **"Sarah was an old, old woman. She laughed when she heard she was going to have a baby. We sometimes laugh when things are funny or we think something is impossible. But nothing is impossible with God."**

10

Here Comes the King

Scripture: Jesus rides into Jerusalem on a donkey (John 12:12-19)

This Game Teaches: We can worship Jesus.

Materials: An 8½-x-11-inch piece of green construction paper for each child

● ● ● ● ● ● ● ● ● ● ● ● ● ● ● ● ●

11

Game: Before the game, decide if you're willing to be a donkey so that a child can ride on your back, or if you need to recruit another willing adult.

Ask for a child volunteer to be Jesus. Give each of the other children a piece of green construction paper. Help the children form two parallel lines with enough room in between so that Jesus can ride the donkey through the middle.

Say: **"In the Bible, there's a story about Jesus riding a donkey into Jerusalem. Everyone along the way held a green plant branch called a palm, and they waved it back and forth as Jesus passed. We're going to do that now. Any questions?"** Have the children practice waving their green paper. Then get on all fours (or have the other adult volunteer do this) and have Jesus climb onto your back. Walk between the two lines of children waving their papers.

Afterward say: **"We should worship Jesus. While we may not have palms to wave, we can sing songs, we can go to church, we can read our Bibles, and we can pray. There are many ways to worship Jesus."**

Where's Moses?

Scripture: Baby Moses in the basket (Exodus 2)
This Game Teaches: People took good care of baby Moses in the basket. We can take good care of one another, too.
Materials: A doll; a doll blanket; a basket for the doll

• • • • • • • • • • • • • • • • •

Game: Wrap the doll in the blanket, and place it in the basket. Hide the doll in the play area. (If there are children present, have them leave the area or close their eyes.)

Say: **"We're going to look for baby Moses, who is hiding. Moses is a baby doll in a basket. Let's all start looking for baby Moses."** Play the game. After the game ends, say: **"The only way baby Moses could be saved was to be placed in a basket and put into the river. But people found baby Moses, and they took good care of him. Moses grew up and became one of God's leaders."**

Ask: **"How can we take good care of one another?"** Give children time to respond.

Say: **"We can take good care of one another like people took care of baby Moses."**

12

Come, Children, Come

Scripture: Jesus blessed the children (Matthew 19:13-15)
This Game Teaches: Every child is blessed by Jesus.
Materials: Two balls

. . . .

13

Game: Before the game, decide if you will be the adult Jesus or if you need to recruit another adult.

Have the children sit in a circle. Say: **"I want you to roll the ball back and forth around the circle. When you hear your name called, leave the circle and go to Jesus. The rest of the children should close the circle."**

Give the adult Jesus the other ball. Explain that you're going to create another circle where children play the same game. Have the Jesus volunteer call the names of the children one at a time. When a child comes to Jesus, the volunteer should say: **"Jesus blesses you"** and lay her or his hands on the child's head. Have the first child in the circle simply sit with the ball. When another child joins the new circle, have the next child (after receiving a blessing) roll the ball back and forth with the other child.

Play the game. Eventually the first circle of children will disappear as the new circle forms. After all the children have been called and had a chance to roll the ball to one another, stop the game.

Then say: **"In Bible times, adults were considered more important than children. But not to Jesus. Everyone is important to Jesus— each one of you. Jesus blesses every child, just as you were blessed today."**

Thanks a Lot!

Scripture: The psalm of thanks (Psalm 107:1)
This Game Teaches: It's good to thank God for everything God gives us.
Materials: None

. . . .

Game: Have the children form a circle. Then have them take four large steps backward so there's a lot of room within the circle. Say: **"The Bible says to give thanks to the Lord. We're going to do that now. Let's go around the circle and take turns clapping and saying the name of someone we're thankful for."** Have the children do that. Then have them go around the circle and do some or all of the following:

- Do a jumping jack and name the food you're most thankful for.
- Sing la, la, la and name the song you're most thankful for.
- Sit down and name the animal you're most thankful for.
- Jump up and name the toy you're most thankful for.
- Turn around in a circle and name the color you're most thankful for.
- Hug the person next to you and name the person you've just hugged.

After the game ends, say: **"It's good to give thanks for everything God has given us: people, animals, food, things to play with, and one another. Thank you, God."**

Lion's Roar

Scripture: Daniel in the lion's den (Daniel 6)
This Game Teaches: The lions didn't hurt Daniel, which was amazing. Even today God keeps us safe.
Materials: None

• • • • • • • • • • • • • • • • • •

15

Game: Have the children get down on the floor and walk around like lions. Tell them to roar like lions when you get near them. Walk among the lions and act scared of their roars.

Then ask for a volunteer to stand up and be Daniel. Tell the children that both you and Daniel will walk around the room. Whenever you come near them, they should roar. Whenever Daniel comes near them, they should purr and brush up against him like a cat.

Afterward say: **"We just played a game of something that really happened in the Bible. A guy named Daniel was thrown into the lion's den. He was very afraid because lions usually ate people who were thrown into the lion's den. But the lions didn't hurt Daniel, which was amazing. Even today God keeps us safe."**

A Welcome Hug

Scripture: The prodigal son (Luke 15:11-20)
This Game Teaches: When we become lost, someone looks for us because we are loved.
Materials: None

• • • • • • • • • • • • • • • • • •

Game: Say: **"We're going to play a game. We will all skip around the room. When I yell out a name of a child, everyone come together and hug the child in a big group hug. When I tell you to skip, go back to skipping. Then I'll name another child, and everybody hug that child. Any questions?"**

16

After the game ends, say: **"In the Bible, there's a story about the prodigal son. The dad was very sad when his son went away. The dad thought the son was lost and would never come back home. But then the son did come back, and the father welcomed the lost son with a great big hug. When we become lost, someone looks for us because we are loved."**

Fill 'er Up

Scripture: The Creation story (Genesis 1–2)

This Game Teaches: God created all kinds of amazing things. We worship an amazing God.

Materials: 8½-x-11-inch pieces of paper in blue, yellow, black, and white; scissors; a computer-paper-size box with a cover; tape; small plastic animals (including some land animals, birds, and sea animals); a small plastic man and woman; a cup of water; pieces of grass or a plant; a handful of dirt; self-adhesive stars (in gold or silver); a room that can be darkened and lightened

• • • • • • • • • • • • • • • • • •

17

Game: Set up the supplies on a table beforehand. Say: **"Today we're going to play the creation game. We're going to pretend we're God and that this box is the world that we create."** Show the empty box with the cover. **"The first thing God created was night and day. Who wants to turn the lights on and off?"** Give the child time to do this. **"On the second**

day, God created the sky and water. Let's make a blue sky on the inside of this cover." Guide the children in taping the blue paper to the inside of the cover. **"Who can walk very carefully and carry the**

cup of water and place it inside the box without spilling it?" As you choose children for various tasks, be intentional about choosing a different child each time.

"On the third day, God created the land and the plants. Let's all stand on our tiptoes and reach toward the sky with our arms as if we are the growing plants. Who will go get

the dirt from the table and who will go get the plants?" Choose children to do this. **"On the fourth day, God made the sun, moon, and stars. I need two people who love to cut circles."** Assign one child to cut a yellow circle and the other to cut a white circle. Sing "Twinkle, Twinkle, Little Star" with the other children as they stick self-adhesive stars onto a piece of black paper. When the children finish cut-

ting the sun (the yellow circle) and the moon (the white circle), tape the moon to the black piece of paper and the sun to the blue piece of paper inside the cover of the box. Tape the black paper to the box and say: **"We now have the nighttime with moon and stars."** Tape the blue paper over the black paper and say: **"And then we have daytime with a sun.**

"On the fifth day, God created the sea creatures and the birds.

Who can get the birds and sea creatures from the pile over there?" Check to ensure that no people or land animals were selected. Have the children add the sea creatures and birds to the box. **"On the sixth day, God created land animals and peo-**

ple. Who will get these from the table?" Have the children add these to the box. Ask each child to name their favorite animal that God made, and to make their animal's sound for the group.

"On the seventh day, God was so tired. Let's all lie on the floor and rest." Have children do this for a short while. End the game by saying: **"Look at what we created!"** Have the children look into the box. **"What do you think of that?"** Give children time to respond. **"God created all kinds of amazing things. We worship an amazing God."**

Awesome Animals

Scripture: Samson sees a lion (Judges 14:5); cows are on the hill (Psalm 50:10); a bird flies from the ark (Genesis 8:6-10); dogs eat leftovers (Matthew 15:27); and pigs eat on the hillside (Mark 5:11)

This Game Teaches: God made many awesome animals.

Materials: None

. . . .

18

Game: Say: **"We can find all kinds of awesome animals throughout the Bible. Let's all get down on the floor and curl up as if we're an egg. When I name an animal, hatch out of that egg. Jump up. Make the noise of that animal and move around the room like that animal until I say 'egg time.' Any questions?"** Practice by having the children act like cats.

Play the game. Mention these scriptures:

- In Judges 14:5, Samson was traveling with his mom and dad. And what did he see? *A lion*.
- In Psalm 50:10, what was on all the hills? *Cows*.
- In Genesis 8:6-10, what did Noah send to look for land? *Birds*.
- In Matthew 15:27, who ate the leftovers from the table? *Dogs*.
- In Mark 5:11, what was eating on the hillside? *Pigs*.

End the game by saying: **"What is your favorite animal that God created?"** Let the children make the sounds of their favorite animal and run around the room. Then say: **"God made many awesome animals. The Bible is full of stories about animals. Let's thank God for all the awesome animals God made."**

Wrong Way, Jonah

Scripture: Jonah and the great fish (Jonah 1–4)
This Game Teaches: God wants us to follow God, not run away.
Materials: A whistle

• • • • • • • • • • • • • • • • •

Game: Have children line up in the middle of the room or play area. Say: **"In the Bible, God wanted Jonah to help some people. God wanted Jonah to go where God wanted, but Jonah always went in the opposite direction. We're going to play a game like that. When I tell you to do something, do the opposite. When I blow the whistle, that means the game is over and you should listen."** Name situations such as these:

- Point to one area of the room and ask children to run in that direction. (They should run in the opposite direction.)
- Stand up. (Children should sit down.)
- Be quiet. (Children should make noise.)
- Don't clap. (Children should clap.)
- Walk, don't run. (Children should run, not walk.)

Stop the game by blowing the whistle. (If you just ask children to stop, they may not, since they're in the mode of doing the opposite.) Play the game again, but this time have children do what you say. Repeat the above list.

After the game ends, say: **"God asked Jonah to do something, but Jonah ran away. Jonah did the opposite of what God wanted him to do. It's much better if we do what God wants us to do. It's good to follow God."**

Send Me!

Scripture: Isaiah accepts God's call (Isaiah 6:8)

This Game Teaches: We can accept God's call, like Isaiah, and follow God.

Materials: A soft-sided tunnel or large box with open ends that's big enough for children to crawl through; a nap mat or large towel; a chair; two adult-size shoe boxes

• • • • • • • • • • • • • • • • •

20

Game: Before playing, set the materials up in a circle to create a circular obstacle course. Put the soft-sided tunnel or large box in one area. Place the nap mat or large towel near by, then add the chair. Put the shoe boxes, side by side with the covers off, between the chair and the tunnel. Allow enough space between each item for the children to maneuver since they will be moving through the obstacle course at the same time.

Say: **"There was a guy named Isaiah in the Bible. God asked, 'Whom should I send?' Isaiah called out, 'Send me!' We're going to play a game like this Bible story."** Demonstrate how children go through the obstacle course. Have them crawl through the tunnel, lie on the nap mat, sit in the chair, then step carefully into the two shoe boxes before starting through the tunnel again.

Say: **"Let's all cluster together off to the side. I'll keep asking, 'Whom shall I send?' Call out your name, saying 'I'm [child's name], send me!' Then be quiet and listen. I will call out one child's name. When I call your name, start crawling through the tunnel and keep going around and around the obstacle course. Do this slowly and watch for other children, since eventually everyone will be going around the course at the same time."**

Call out: **"Whom shall I send?"** Pick a child by saying his or her name. Pause. Then ask again: **"Whom shall I send?"** Pick another child by naming that child. The children named should start going through the obstacle course. Keep calling out names until all the children are playing the game.

Afterward say: **"We can accept God's call, like Isaiah, and follow God. Sometimes following God will seem like a lot of work, like going through this obstacle course, but it's good to follow God."**

A Single Touch

Scripture: A woman who touches Jesus' robe is healed (Mark 5:25-34)

This Game Teaches: Jesus was so powerful that a single touch from him could heal people. We have a powerful God.

Materials: An adult-size bathrobe (long enough to drag on the floor)

• • • • • • • • • • • • • • • • •

Game: Say: **"In the Bible, there's a story about a sick woman. We're going to act like that sick woman. I want you to all sit on the floor."** Ask for a volunteer to be Jesus, and put the bathrobe on the volunteer. **"Jesus is going to walk around the room. You can reach out and try to touch the robe, but you cannot stand up or move toward it. When you touch the robe, jump up and say, 'I'm well!' When everyone is well, the game is done. Any questions?"** Demonstrate how this works by having Jesus walk and one of the children touch the robe and jump up to say "I'm well." Then play the game.

After the game ends, say: **"Jesus was so powerful that a single touch from him could heal people. We follow a powerful God."**

Hooray!
David's the King!

Scripture: David becomes king (2 Samuel 5:1-5)
This Game Teaches: It's important to celebrate when good
  things happen.
Materials: Paper plates; dried beans; stapler; markers

• • • • • • • • • • • • • • • • •

22

Game: Before playing the game, have children create tambourines. First have them decorate the bottom sides of two paper plates with markers. Then help them put dried beans in between the two plates and staple the plates together with the colored sides facing out. Finally, have them practice shaking their tambourines.

Then say: **"Let's celebrate. Listen closely to what I have to say. Then do the actions that I say. Ready?"** Name actions, such as these:

- Shake your tambourine.
- Dance and shake your tambourine.
- Toss your tambourine in the air and catch it.
- Tap your tambourine with the tambourine of the child next to you.
- Jump up and down while shaking your tambourine.
- Let's sing "I've Got the Joy, Joy, Joy, Down in My Heart" as we walk around the room and shake our tambourines.

After the game ends, say: **"It's important to celebrate when good things happen, like when we have birthdays and holidays. When David became king in the Bible, people danced and sang and shook tambourines."**

Shoes Off!

Scripture: The burning bush (Exodus 3:1-6)
This Game Teaches: It's important to be yourself with God.
Materials: A potted plant (the bigger, the better)

• • • • • • • • • • • • • • • • • •

Game: Set a potted plant in the middle of the room, and have the children form a circle around it. Have each child take five steps backward. Say: **"We're going to pretend we're Moses today. God spoke to Moses through a bush, like this plant."** Point to the plant. **"When I say a color, look at your socks or tights. If that's the color I called, run up to the plant, take off both of your shoes, and then run back to the circle. Any questions?"**

23

Play the game. Take note of the color of socks and tights of the children. Common colors to call out include *black, blue, white, gray,* and *pink.* After the game ends, have children find their shoes and put them on. Say: **"When God spoke to Moses through the bush, God asked Moses to take off his shoes. That's what we did today. God wants us to be ourselves. Taking off our shoes is a way to follow what God wants us to do while also being ourselves."**

Little and Big

Scripture: Zacchaeus climbs a tree (Luke 19:1-10)
This Game Teaches: We're all to follow Jesus, whether we're little or big.
Materials: A sturdy chair for a child to stand on

• • • • • • • • • • • • • • • • •

24

Game: Ask for two volunteers. Have one be Jesus and sit on the floor. Invite the other to be Zacchaeus and stand next to you for the moment—away from Jesus. Ask the other children to stand around the sitting Jesus. Place the chair behind one of the standing children.

Then say: **"There was a little man named Zacchaeus."** Have the child acting as Zacchaeus get down on her or his knees to become shorter than the standing kids. **"Zacchaeus wanted to see Jesus. But Zacchaeus was little. Even when he tried to see over the crowd, he couldn't see."** Encourage Zacchaeus to move around the outside of the circle on her or his knees.

"Then Zacchaeus saw a tree." Point out the chair. Encourage Zacchaeus to climb onto the chair and stand. Stand beside her or him to ensure the child does not fall. **"From the tree, Zacchaeus could see. But do you know who else could see? Jesus could see. Jesus saw Zacchaeus and asked him to come down. Jesus was happy that little Zacchaeus wanted to follow him. We're all to follow Jesus, whether we're little or big."**

Hugs and Laughs

Scripture: "How we laughed, how we sang for joy!" (Psalm 126:2*a* TEV)

This Game Teaches: We can love. We can laugh. We can have fun.

Materials: None

• • • • • • • • • • • • • • • • •

Game: Have the children stand and spread out. Say: **"We're going to play a hugging game. Listen closely and hug what I say. Any questions?"**

Call out items and people to hug such as these:

- Hug your foot.
- Hug your nose.
- Hug one person.
- Hug a tree (if you're playing outside).
- Hug yourself.
- Hug your belly button.
- Hug your lips.
- Hug two people.
- Now hug me!

After the game ends, say: **"We can love. We can hug. We can laugh. We can have fun. It's good to come together at church."**

Great Games for GRADES K-3

A s children enter elementary school, they become more capable of playing games that have a set of rules and guidelines. Even with this new capacity, however, rules and guidelines need to be simple and few. Whereas "Follow the Leader" is a classic game for preschoolers (since children are given one instruction at a time while following the example of a leader), games such as "Red Light, Green Light" and "Simon Says" stimulate young elementary children because they require slightly more complex thinking skills that they find challenging.

Because following rules and guidelines is new for children at this age, they also are apt to change them, particularly if the changes give them an advantage. If you give first- and second-graders full control of a game, they often can become frustrated when several of the players begin to independently change the rules as the game goes on. That's why it's important to go over the rules and guidelines before playing a particular game so that everyone *understands* and *agrees* with the rules.

Children in the primary grades enjoy using their imagination, just like preschoolers, but they're more likely to focus their efforts on developing individual skills, such as kicking a rolled ball, hopping on one foot, skipping, or sliding into a base. A simple game of toss and catch is often a challenging and enjoyable game for children at this age. They love it when they can play games at which they can succeed.

49

Tongue Tips

Scripture: The following scriptures that name specific colors:
Zechariah 6:2; Jeremiah 22:14; Nahum 2:3; Revelation 9:17;
Hosea 14:8; Genesis 9:3; Joel 2:22; Luke 23:31; Exodus 26:36;
2 Chronicles 2:7; Esther 1:6; Genesis 9:16

This Game Teaches: God made all colors. We can thank God
for making a colorful world.

Materials: Three packages of unprepared, presweetened
powdered drink mix: one in red, one in blue, one in green

• • • • • • • • • • • • • • • • •

26

Game: Form three groups. Give each group a different color
of unprepared drink mix: red, blue, or green. Have children
each put a little bit of drink mix on their tongues until their
tongues turn that color. Have the children mingle and mix up.
Then have them sit in a circle.

Say: **"We're going to see how many ways colors are used in the
Bible. When I name your color, stick out your tongue. Pull it
back in when the next color is called. Any questions?"**

Use these color descriptions:

- Zechariah 6:2 talks about red horses.
- Hosea 14:8 talks about green pine trees.
- Exodus 26:36 tells of a blue curtain.
- Genesis 9:3 tells of green plants.
- 2 Chronicles 2:7 talks about blue yarn.
- Jeremiah 22:14 talks about putting up walls in a house and painting them red.
- Esther 1:6 tells about blue linen.
- Nahum 2:3 tells about red soldier shields.
- Joel 2:22 talks about green pastures.
- Revelation 9:17 tells about breastplates that are as red as fire and as blue as sapphire.
- Luke 23:31 tells of green trees.
- Genesis 9:16 talks about all the colors of the rainbow.

After the game ends, say: **"God made all the colors, and they're
all important colors. Every time we see a color, we can thank
God for making colors for us."**

Where's Joseph?

Scripture: Joseph being sold by his brothers (Genesis 37:12-28)
This Game Teaches: People can recognize us just by looking at a piece of our clothing. When people found the amazing, colorful coat, they knew it belonged to Joseph.
Materials: A colorful coat or robe and a room or field with lots of good hiding places

• • • • • • • • • • • • • • • • •

Game: Ask for a volunteer to be Joseph. Say: **"We're going to play a game about the Bible story that talks about Joseph and his amazing, colorful coat."** Put the colorful coat or robe on the child who volunteered. **"Everyone go to the other end of the room, line up, and cover your eyes. While I count aloud to forty, Joseph will take off his coat, drop it, and find a place to hide. When I get to forty, go to the coat and say, 'Oh no! Joseph's missing!' Then spread out and look for Joseph. The child who finds Joseph first gets to be Joseph the next time."**

After the children have lined up, start the game. Repeat the activity as many times as you wish.

Afterward say: **"People can recognize us just by looking at a piece of our clothing. When people found the amazing, colorful coat, they knew it belonged to Joseph."**

Watch Out for That Light!

Scripture: Saul's conversion (Acts 9:1-19)
This Game Teaches: Anyone can follow God—even people who we think are evil.
Materials: A room that can be darkened; a flashlight

• • • • • • • • • • • • • • • • •

28

Game: Ask for a volunteer. Give the child a flashlight, and say he or she gets to play God in this game. Explain that the child is to select a spot in the room and play the entire game from there. The only thing the child can move is the flashlight, by having the light dance around the room until he or she selects a person and shines the light on him or her.

Say: **"The rest of us are going to be people who are walking on the road to Damascus. As we walk, we don't know which one of us is going to have the light from the flashlight pick us out by flashing on us. If that happens to you, fall to the ground and say, 'I am Saul. Who are you?' God will then say, 'I am God.' Then we'll walk again and another child will be chosen with the flashlight. Then the game ends. Any questions? Let's begin."**

Play the game. Let the child with the flashlight shine it on one child before playing again by shining it on a second child. Repeat the game a few times so different children have the chance to be chosen or to shine the flashlight. After the game ends, say: **"Saul was a bad guy before he met up with God on the road to Damascus. Saul was trying to kill Christians. But once the light came and blinded him, Saul changed his ways. He became a follower of God. Anyone can follow God—even people who we think are evil. People can change and do good things."**

Snakebites

Scripture: Moses makes a metal snake (Numbers 21:4-9)
This Game Teaches: Healing can occur when we get hurt.
Materials: A warm day; sidewalk or asphalt; chalk; a plastic snake (or a snake drawn on paper); duct tape

● ● ● ● ● ● ● ● ● ● ● ● ● ● ● ● ● ●

Game: Take the children outside. Hang the snake from a tree or wall. Give children chalk and have them draw a long, fat snake on the asphalt or sidewalk. Collect the chalk when they finish.

Say: **"We're going to play a game. In the Old Testament when a snake bit someone, that person often died. So Moses made a healing snake, like our snake over there.** (Point to the hanging snake.) **To play the game, we are going to run around this chalk-drawn snake on the ground. When I yell 'snakebite' run into the mouth of the chalk-drawn snake and down its body as if you're being eaten. When you get to the tail, run to the hanging snake and look at it to get healed. Then come back and run around the snake until I yell 'snakebite' again. Any questions?"**

Play the game a number of times. After the game ends, say: **"When we get hurt, we can get better. We can be healed. When we fall and scrape our knees, we often put a bandage on it and it hurts for a while. But then it heals and gets better. The hanging snake in Moses' time was a healing snake. When people were bitten, they looked at the hanging snake, and they got better."**

Walking Without Sinking

Scripture: Jesus walks on the water (Matthew 14:22-33)
This Game Teaches: Christ is there for us, to calm the
  storms, to calm our fears.
Materials: None

. . . .

Game: Ask for a volunteer to be Jesus. Send Jesus to the
other side of the room to pray on an imaginary hill. Ask for
another volunteer, and have that person be Peter.

Have Peter and the rest of the children stand together and
pretend they're in a boat. Encourage them to pretend to row the
boat and to bob slightly up and down. Say: **"There's a storm coming, but there isn't time to get the boat to shore. Oh my, it's really
getting wavy. Up and down. Up and down. Ride the waves. And
hang on."** Encourage the children to exaggerate the up and down
movement.

"Now it's really stormy. Hang on to the edges. Hang on to each other. It looks like the waves are going to crash the boat." Encourage the children to exaggerate their fears. Then motion for Jesus to come slowly toward them.

"But what's this? Who is walking on the water? Who is walking on top of the crashing waves?" Encourage the children to scream and say, "It's a ghost! It's a ghost!"

Have Jesus identify himself. Then have Peter challenge him, saying something like, "Jesus, if it's really you, have me come out onto the water." Have Jesus agree, and have Peter crawl out of the boat. Encourage Peter to walk a few steps and then start to bend his knees, like he's sinking. Have Peter call out for help. Have Jesus go to Peter and take his hand.

"Peter and Jesus got into the boat." Pause to let the two children get into the boat. "Then the storm stopped. Everything was calm. The disciples were amazed at what Jesus had done."

After the game say: "Although it's easy to focus only on the miracle and power of Jesus in this story, what's as important is the fact that we need to believe in God—even when our lives get hard and stormy. Christ is there for us, to calm the storms, to calm our fears."

Who's Hidden?

Scripture: Aunt Jehosheba hides her nephew Joash (2 Kings 11:1-3)

This Game Teaches: When you're in danger, you can find people to take care of you.

Materials: None

• • • • • • • • • • • • • • • • • •

31. **Game:** Say: **"We're going to play a guessing game. When I tell you to, spread out around the room, duck your head, and close your eyes. I'll walk around the room and tap two different people. Those two children will quietly leave the room. Don't peek when you hear movement because the fun of this game is trying to figure out who left. Any questions? Okay, everyone spread out, duck your head, and close your eyes."**

Choose two children to leave the room. After they leave, have everyone open their eyes and gather together. Ask the children to figure out which two children left the room. When the two children have been correctly identified, invite them back into the room. Then play the game again, choosing two different children.

After the game ends, say:

"In 2 Kings 11, a little boy was in danger. His name was Joash. Joash's aunt hid him until it was safe. The two of them hid together for six years. When we're in danger, we can find people to take care of us. Aunt Jehosheba took care of Joash, just as our parents, family, and friends take care of us."

Run, Run, Run

Scripture: Running to the empty tomb (John 20:3-4)

This Game Teaches: When we know where we want to go and we want to get there fast, it's amazing how fast we can run, just like Mary at the empty tomb.

Materials: None

• • • • • • • • • • • • • • • • •

Game: Have children form a circle and stand an arm's length apart. Ask a volunteer to stand in the middle. Say: **"The person in the middle is going to try to run out of the circle by running between two children. Those in the circle can move to the right and the left to make it hard for the runner to slip through. But, if the runner does get through, the two children whom the runner slipped between must chase the runner around the circle. The last one to get around the circle will be the next child in the center."** Encourage children not to roughly break through the circle, since the point is to try to slip through a space before children close it. Demonstrate how to slip through a space with the children before playing the game.

After the game say: **"When Mary discovered the empty tomb, she ran to the disciples and told them the news. Then the disciples ran as fast as they could to find out what had happened. All the disciples didn't reach the tomb at the same time because some ran faster than others. When we know where we want to go and we want to get there fast, it's amazing how fast we can run."**

Finding Ruth in the Field

Scripture: Boaz meets Ruth in the field (Ruth 2)

This Game Teaches: Boaz finds Ruth in the field and becomes her friend. We can meet new people and become friends.

Materials: Five to six identical stickers

• • • • • • • • • • • • • • • • • •

33

Game: Ask for one volunteer to be Boaz. Have Boaz leave the room for a moment, and ask for a second volunteer. Put a sticker on the front of the child's shirt or dress. Call this child Ruth.

Say: **"We're going to play a game about Ruth and Boaz. When Boaz returns, he's going to be looking for Ruth, who is the child wearing the sticker. Everyone is going to pretend they're working in a field, bent over, picking strawberries. As quietly as you can, count aloud to five. When you reach five, stand up quickly and then hunch down and act as if you're picking strawberries again. Begin counting and do the same motion again. Okay? Let's get all hunched over and pretend to pick. I'll tell you when to start counting."**

Invite Boaz back into the room. Say: **"We're playing a game about Ruth and Boaz. Since you're Boaz, you're supposed to find Ruth, who is one of these children. You can walk around and through the children, but you cannot bend over to see who Ruth is. Ruth is wearing a sticker on her shirt**. (Show one of the extra identical stickers.) **Every so often, the children will stand up so you can see what's on their chest. When you see Ruth, shout out 'I've found Ruth!' Point to the correct child. The game will then end. Okay, everyone, let's begin."**

Play the game. If time permits, repeat the game a number of times so other children have a chance to be Ruth and Boaz. After the game say: **"Boaz found Ruth in the field and became her friend. As we get to know new people, we can become friends with them, too."**

I Say Go, I Say No

Scripture: Peter and Paul in prison (Acts 12:6-17; 16:16-40)
This Game Teaches: We need to follow God, even when we don't understand.
Materials: A large play area

• • • • • • • • • • • • • • • • •

Game: Ask for a volunteer to be the angel. Tell the child to stand at one end of the play area and use a loud voice during the game. Have all the other children line up and stand at the opposite end of the play area.

Say: **"We're going to play a game like Simon Says. In this game, the angel over there will raise her (or his) arm straight into the air and say 'Go' when you're supposed to go. Walk when you hear the word 'go.' When the angel lowers her (or his) arm and puts it straight out in front like a stop motion and says 'No,' stop wherever you are. The angel will continue to say 'Go' and 'No' until everyone reaches the angel. Any questions?"**

Play the game. Afterward say: **"In Acts 12, Peter was in prison. An angel came and said 'Go,' so Peter got up and walked right out of prison with the angel. In Acts 16, Paul was in prison with Silas. An earthquake came and shook open the doors and chains. Now, Paul could have gone, but he followed God and knew the answer was 'no.' Paul and Silas knew they had to stay even though the doors were opened and it would have been easy for them to leave. We need to follow God, even when we don't understand."**

There He Goes!

Scripture: A chariot of fire takes Elijah to heaven (2 Kings 2)

This Game Teaches: Even though he knew something hard was about to happen, Elisha stayed with Elijah. It's good to stick together during difficulties.

Materials: A bath-sized towel; seven children

• • • • • • • • • • • • • • • • • •

35

Game: Ask for two volunteers. Name one Elijah and give her or him the towel to drape over his shoulder. Name the other child Elisha. Tell the rest of the children that they are going to be the horses.

Say: **"Before we play this game, let me tell you the story of Elijah and Elisha. Pay close attention to what I say because later I want you to act out your part. Ready?**

"Elijah and Elisha traveled together. Elijah was old, and Elisha was going to take Elijah's place. When Elijah got to the river Jordan, he took his cloak (take the towel from the child's shoulders) **and beat the water. The water divided and the two walked to the other side. Suddenly a chariot with horses appeared, and Elijah was taken away to the heavens. But as he left, Elijah dropped his cloak.** (Drop the towel on the ground.) **After Elijah left, Elisha picked up the cloak** (pick up the towel) **and cried. But then he walked back to the river and asked God to help him. He hit the water, and the water divided. Elisha walked through the dry path alone."** Pause for a moment. Then say: **"Let's play the game. When it's time for the horses to come, I want those children to surround Elijah and pick him up and carry him across the room. Any questions?"** Give the towel back to Elijah. Begin the game, and prompt the children about what they need to do next by telling the story aloud.

After the game say: **"Before Elijah and Elisha got to the water, Elisha was told a number of times what was going to happen. Many times Elijah told Elisha to stay back, but Elisha wanted to be with Elijah. Even though he knew something hard was about to happen, Elisha stayed with Elijah. Although it's exciting that Elijah was taken to heaven by the horses, it was sad for Elisha. He missed Elijah. So even when life gets hard, it's good to stick together."**

Important Visitors

Scripture: Those who visited baby Jesus (Luke 2:1-20 and Matthew 2:1-2)
This Game Teaches: Everyone is important.
Materials: None

• • • • • • • • • • • • • • • • • •

Game: Count off children by fours. Tell the *ones* they're sheep, the *twos* they're shepherds, the *threes* they're wise men, and the *fours* they're camels. As a reminder, ask each child which he or she is to make sure the children all understand their roles.

Have the children spread out around the room. Say that when you call a certain grouping, the children in that group should run to the middle, form a circle by holding hands, and walk around the circle once. When they finish walking, they should spread out around the room again.

Call out these groupings:

• Animals (sheep and camels)
• People (shepherds and wise men)
• Shepherds and sheep
• Wise men and camels
• Those who came to see baby Jesus (everybody)

After the game ends, say: **"Everyone was important to Jesus—the people and the animals. Everyone who came to see baby Jesus was important. We're important, too. Each one of us is important to Jesus."**

Gather and Scatter

Scripture: A time for everything (Ecclesiastes 3:1, 4-5*a* NIV)
This Game Teaches: There is a time for everything.
Materials: Two or three bags of cotton balls

• • • • • • • • • • • • • • • •

37

Game: Scatter all the cotton balls around the room. Say: **"We're going to play a game called 'Gather and Scatter.' When I tell you to gather, start picking up as many cotton balls as you can. When I tell you to scatter, throw the balls you're holding into the air. Any questions?"**

Play the game, alternating the instructions between gather and scatter a number of times. Afterward read aloud Ecclesiastes 3:1, 4-5*a*, using the New International Version or another version that uses the words "gathering" and "scattering stones" in verse 5*a*.

Then say: **"There is a time for everything. Sometimes we will feel sad, other times happy. Sometimes we will feel that everything is going right, other times that everything is going wrong. Sometimes we will want to be with people, sometimes we won't. This is all part of what it means to be human. But no matter what we feel, we can always talk to God— and one another."**

Have Faith and Jump

Scripture: Jesus heals Bartimaeus (Mark 10:46-52)
This Game Teaches: Faith can take us to new places.
Materials: Two overcoats; a large playing area

• • • • • • • • • • • • • • • • •

Game: Create two teams with an equal number of children. If an odd number of children are present, have one child be Jesus. If the teams are equally divided, you be Jesus.

Have the teams each form a single line, and sit down. Give the first person in each line a coat to put on. Station Jesus about eight feet away from the two lines, in the middle so that he or she is about the same distance from the first person on each team.

Say: **"We're going to play a game. When I say to begin, the first person in line must jump up, take off the coat, run to Jesus, and kneel. Jesus puts a hand on the child's head and says, 'You're healed.' Then the healed child must run back to the team and tag the next person in line so that child can do exactly what the first child did. The next person in line can put on the coat right away but must wait to be tagged before running to Jesus. The game ends when everyone has been healed by Jesus. Any questions?"**

Play the game. After the game ends, say: **"Faith can take us to new places. In Mark 10, a blind man named Bartimaeus jumped up and threw off his coat when he heard Jesus was nearby. Jesus healed Bartimaeus because Bartimaeus had faith. When we have faith and believe—even when it seems as if what we believe in is impossible, amazing things can happen."**

38

Fantastic Fingers

Scripture: David considers the work of God's fingers—the heavens, the moon, and the stars (Psalm 8:3 NIV)

This Game Teaches: God created amazing things with God's fingers.

Materials: A yellow and a white jelly bean for each child and one extra set; other jelly beans for a snack; a large playing area; masking tape

• • • • • • • • • • • • • • • • • •

39

Game: Create two teams with an equal number of children on each team. If you have an odd number of children, ask a volunteer to do the activity twice. Use masking tape to mark a line on the floor about six feet away from the beginning of the two teams.

Form two lines as you would set up for a relay. Give each child a white jelly bean. Have everyone kneel. Say: **"When we begin the game, the first person in line sets the white jelly bean on the floor and can move it only with her or his fingers. You can only crawl, but you can use your fingers in any way you'd like. You need to get the jelly bean past the masking tape line and then back to your team. Then the second person can go. When you finish your turn, move to the back of the line, get a yellow jelly bean, and do the same thing when it's your turn. Any questions?"**

Play the game. After the game ends, have children throw away the jelly beans they rolled on the floor. Give children other jelly beans to eat for a snack. Show the white and yellow jelly beans you set aside. Read aloud Psalm 8:3. Say: **"The white jelly bean reminds me of the moon. The yellow jelly bean reminds me of the stars. I think it's amazing what God created with God's fingers."**

Follow Me

Scripture: Jesus calls Matthew to be a disciple (Matthew 9:9)
This Game Teaches: Jesus called followers—and leaders.
Materials: None

• • • • • • • • • • • • • • • • •

40

Game: Have children stand in a circle. Say: **"We're going to sing a Bible song that we all know. Who would like to choose the song?** (Select someone and have that person choose the song.) **Now we're going to play a game. First we will hold hands in a circle. Then we will walk around as we sing the song. When I say 'stop,' stop singing and walking, and drop each other's hands. Then point to someone else in the circle. The person with the most fingers pointing at her or him will be Matthew. That person will get into the middle of the circle and lead the group in two actions that he or she chooses. Next, the person will join the circle again and name a song he or she would like sung. Then everyone will hold hands and play the game again."**

Practice playing the game once to demonstrate how it works. Then play the game a few times. Afterward say: **"Jesus called twelve people to be his disciples. Not only were they good followers of Jesus, but they also were good leaders. They also had to lead the people. As Christians, we need to be good followers and good leaders."**

Birds and a Brook

Scripture: Ravens bring food, and a brook gives water to Elijah (1 Kings 17:1-6)

This Game Teaches: God takes care of us in unexpected ways sometimes.

Materials: Two clothespins; two large black bath towels (or black capes); paper cups; a pitcher of water; crackers

• • • • • • • • • • • • • • • • • •

Game: Ask for two volunteers and give each person a black towel or cape. Use a clothespin to secure the towel like a cape. Give each child a cracker to hold. Tell them that they are the ravens, and encourage them to pretend to fly when you ask them to move.

Ask for another volunteer. Give that child a paper cup with some water in it, and tell her or him to be a brook. Enlist one more volunteer to sit in the middle of the floor and be Elijah. Have the other children sit and watch.

Say: **"We're going to act out the story in 1 Kings 17. In that story, Elijah tells the king that there will be no rain for two or three years. Then God tells Elijah to hide.** (Motion for Elijah to hide.) **Even though Elijah was in hiding, God took care of him. Every day, ravens came and brought Elijah food.** (Signal for the ravens to bring Elijah crackers.) **Every day a brook brought Elijah water.** (Signal for the child with the cup to bring Elijah water.) **Although other people didn't have water and food, Elijah did because God took care of him."**

After the game ends, say: **"God takes care of us in unexpected ways sometimes. Although the other brooks dried up, one brook kept bringing water for Elijah. And although many of the animals and birds probably died because of the drought, ravens brought Elijah food every morning and every night."**

Lots of Letters

Scripture: Paul's Letter to Philemon (Philemon)

This Game Teaches: Certain words are important words of the Christian faith. They teach us how to live.

Materials: Several 8½-x-11-inch pieces of paper; lots of pencils; three tables for writing; lots of rubber bands; tape; a container (such as a box, bucket, or basket)

• • • • • • • • • • • • • • • • •

Game: Prior to playing the game, create three writing stations. Place the 8½-x-11-inch paper, pencils, and rubber bands at each station. Write the word "God" on one piece of paper, and tape it to the middle of one table. Write the word "Joy" on another piece of paper, and tape it to the middle of the next table. Write the word "Love" on a third piece of paper,

42

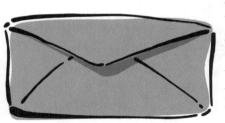

and tape it to the middle of the last table. Place the container far away from the three tables.

Say: **"We're going to pretend that we're Paul in the Bible. When I tell you to begin, everyone run to a table. You can choose any table to run to first. Write the word you see written in the middle of the table. When you finish, roll up your paper like this.** (Show how you roll a sheet of paper into a scroll.) **Place a rubber band around it.** (Demonstrate.) **Then run to the container and drop it in.** (Demonstrate this.) **After you finish, run to one of the other two stations and do the same thing. You'll end the game when you have written all three words and dropped them into the box. Any questions?"**

Begin the game. Be sensitive to kindergartners and children who may have trouble writing letters. Encourage them to do their best and assist them if needed. After the game ends, say: **"The Bible is full of important words like 'God,' 'love,' and 'joy.' Paul used these words when he wrote his letters. These are important words for people to know—even today."**

Turn, Kneel, Bow

Scripture: Kneel only before the one true God
(Isaiah 45:22-23)
This Game Teaches: We should worship only God.
Materials: None

• • • • • • • • • • • • • • • • • •

43

Game: Before playing the game, practice the following motions from a walking position:

- Kneel
- Turn
- A Bow

Say: **"Now that we know these motions, we're going to play a game. Start out by walking around the room. Listen closely and do the action I call out. When I tell you that it's okay to walk again, walk and listen for the next action. Any questions?"**

Call out the three commands, "kneel," "turn," and "bow," mixing up their order, sometimes saying them more quickly and other times more slowly. After the game say: **"Isaiah 45 says that we should worship only the one true God. That means we should turn toward God. And it means we should kneel and bow only before God, not other gods. Turning, kneeling, and bowing are important ways people worshiped God in the Bible."**

Caring Cornelius

Scripture: Cornelius helps the poor (Acts 10:1-4)
This Game Teaches: God is pleased when we help others.
Materials: Play money; bandages; blankets; toy doctor's kit (optional)

. . . .

Game: Form two groups of children. One group will represent the poor. Have them spread out throughout the room either lying or sitting on the floor. The other group represents Cornelius. Give this group play money, bandages, blankets, and a toy doctor's kit (if available).

Say: **"Cornelius was a very caring man, and he helped those who needed help. Those of you pretending to be Cornelius, go help the poor. You can give them play money. You can put bandages on their pretend sores. You can put blankets on them if you think they're cold. Do whatever you think would help them."** Play the game.

Afterward say: **"Cornelius helped a lot of poor people. After he had been doing this for a while, an angel came to Cornelius and told him how pleased God was with the way he helped other people. We can help people, too. When we help others, God likes that."**

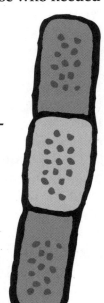

44

Rebuilding the Wall

Scripture: Rebuilding Jerusalem (Nehemiah 2:11-18 and 6:15)
This Game Teaches: Even if something looks like it is completely ruined, it can be rebuilt.
Materials: Building blocks, cardboard boxes, or other materials to build a wall

• • • • • • • • • • • • • • • • • •

45

Game: Gather materials for building a wall and have the children dump them onto the floor and make a mess. Then have everyone gather in an area away from the materials.

Ask the children to become very quiet. Say that everyone is going to investigate the wall in secret. Together, tiptoe to the mess. Ask the children what they see. Encourage them to whisper or use quiet voices to answer. Then say: **"We're going to be like Nehemiah. We're going to build a wall from this big mess!"** Have the children build a wall.

After the game say: **"Sometimes it looks as though we have a complete mess on our hands and that everything is ruined. That may happen with an art project, learning a sport, or having to clean our bedroom. Nehemiah couldn't believe it when he saw the walls of Jerusalem ruined. But he knew the walls could be built again. So the people went to work, and the walls were rebuilt."**

Blind Leading the Blind

Scripture: Blind leading the blind (Matthew 15:14)
This Game Teaches: It's important to stick with and learn from Christians.
Materials: Two blindfolds

• • • • • • • • • • • • • • • • •

Game: Form two groups with about the same number of children in each group. Have each group form a single line, with the two lines parallel to each other and about four feet apart. Ask for two volunteers. Blindfold and place them between the two lines.

Say: **"We're going to play a game about blindness. This child** (designate one of the blindfolded children) **is going to lead this child** (the other blindfolded child) **by moving through the line and holding the child's hand. Everyone else is to keep the two children safe while they do this by holding out your arms and guiding them back if they start to get off course. Even though they are not supposed to see where they are going, we don't want them bumping into things and getting hurt."**

Begin the game. When the two children reach the other end of the area, stop the game for a moment. Take off the blindfold of the leader child. Have the two children walk back through the line again with the leader being able to see. When they finish, ask questions such as: **"Which was easier? Why? Do you think it's a good idea for the blind to lead the blind? Why or why not?"**

After the game ends, say: **"When Jesus was talking about the blind leading the blind, he was talking about non-Christians following non-Christians. How can you learn about God when you don't go to church? It's like the blind leading the blind. Instead, we'll be able to see God and live our lives much more clearly when we go to church and have friends who are Christians."**

Stew for Supper

Scripture: Elisha makes the poisoned stew safe (2 Kings 4:38-41)

This Game Teaches: When there's a problem, talk about it and someone can help.

Materials: A large box; an empty wrapping paper roll; a bag of cotton balls; one colored cotton ball (To make a colored ball soak a cotton ball in food coloring and let it dry.)

• • • • • • • • • • • • • • • •

47

Game: Set the large box in the middle of the room. Put the wrapping paper roll inside it so that one end sticks out. Give each child a cotton ball. Give one child a colored cotton ball. Tell the child with the colored ball that he or she is Elisha.

Say: **"Let's gather around the box and pretend it's a pot of stew. Let's take turns stirring the stew.** (Give one child the end of the empty wrapping paper roll and have her or him pretend to stir the stew.) **Now, we each have something to put into the stew. Think of healthy foods that you'd like to put into the stew.** (Choose a child to begin.) **When it's your turn, throw your cotton ball into the stew, and say the name of one healthy food that you're putting into the stew. Any questions?"** Play the game. Have the child with the colored cotton ball wait to use her or his ball. The game can also be started by throwing in a cotton ball yourself and naming a food, such as onions, garlic, potatoes, apples, etc.

When the children have added in their ingredients, say: **"The stew is poisoned! We can't eat it! What are we going to do?"** Pause for a moment. **"Elisha can help us. Elisha, do you have something to put into the stew?"** Let Elisha throw the colored cotton ball in the stew. Use the stirring stick and pretend to taste the stew. Let the children pretend to taste it also. **"The stew is good now. It's safe! Elisha saved the stew."**

After the game ends, say: **"When there's a problem, we need to talk about it and often someone can help. In 2 Kings, the people were so hungry. They wanted to eat the stew, but it was poisoned. But when they talked about it, Elisha knew what to do. Elisha saved the stew!"**

Who Did What?

Scripture: Mary and Martha (Luke 10:38-42)
This Game Teaches: It's important to take time to learn about God.
Materials: None

• • • • • • • • • • • • • • • •

Game: Number children by fours. Tell the *ones* they're Mary, the *twos* they're Martha, the *threes* they're disciples, and the *fours* they're Jesus. Ask each child who he or she is to ensure that everyone understands their role. Encourage children to pay close attention to the person they represent during the game as you read the scripture aloud. Read Luke 10:38-42.

Have the children spread out around the room and take a seat. Tell them that when you call a certain group, the children in that group should jump up and say, "Jesus knows what's best" while turning around in a circle. When they finish, they should sit back down.

Call out these groupings:

• Who came to Martha and Mary's house? *(Jesus and the disciples)*
• Who sat at Jesus' feet? *(Mary)*
• Who was upset about someone not helping her with the work? *(Martha)*
• Who came with Jesus to the house? *(the disciples)*
• Who are the women? *(Mary and Martha)*
• Who did all the teaching? *(Jesus)*
• Who did all the work? *(Martha)*
• Who are the men? *(Jesus and the disciples)*
• Which woman did Jesus say chose the right thing to do? *(Mary)*

After the game say: **"Although there was a lot to do, Jesus praised Mary for making the choice to take time to hear what he had to say. The best choice would have been if both Martha and Mary had stopped their work to learn from Jesus and then gone back to work together. It's good to learn what Jesus has to tell us."**

Rain, What Rain?

Scripture: God sends rain to one field but not another (Amos 4:7)

This Game Teaches: Plants need rain to grow.

Materials: One spray bottle filled with water; a hot, sunny day; permission for children to get wet

· · · · · · · · · · · · · · · · · ·

49

Game: Ask parents for permission to get children wet. Children whose parents don't agree, can stay in the drought area of the game. Take the children outside, and ask for a volunteer. Give that person a spray bottle, and say: **"This is the rain. If you run into this area,** (point to a specific area) **you could get rained on. If you stay in this area,** (point to another area) **you will never get wet because that area is having a drought."** Make sure the person with the spray bottle is clear about the two areas and will make rain only by spraying at children from the neck down. Then play the game.

Afterward say: **"We had a lot of fun with the water, but if we were plants, we would feel differently. How would we feel if we were in the field that never got any rain? What would happen? How would we feel if we were in the field that always got rain? What would happen? Plants need rain to grow, but they need the right amount—not too much and not too little, which is what happened in Amos 4."**

Paul's Far Journeys

Scripture: Paul travels to Arabia, Damascus, Jerusalem, Syria, Cilicia, and many other places (Galatians 1:17-21)
This Game Teaches: Paul traveled to many places to tell people about God. Children can tell others about God, too.
Materials: A large play area with different places that children can run to

• • • • • • • • • • • • • • • • •

Game: Before playing this game, clear the area so children can run safely. Make note of items that children can run to. For example, if playing indoors, items might include a chalkboard, door, window, bookcase, table, and so on. If playing outside, items might include a trash receptacle, tree, swing set, fence, and so forth.

Say: **"We're going to play a running game. When I call out an object, run to it as fast as you can. After everyone gets there, I'll name another object. Run to it. Keep doing this until the game ends."**

Play the game. Afterward say: **"You really went to a lot of places. You're probably very tired. Paul, too, went to many places. The Bible tells about him traveling to Arabia, Damascus, Jerusalem, Syria, and many other places to tell others about God. We can tell others about God, too."**

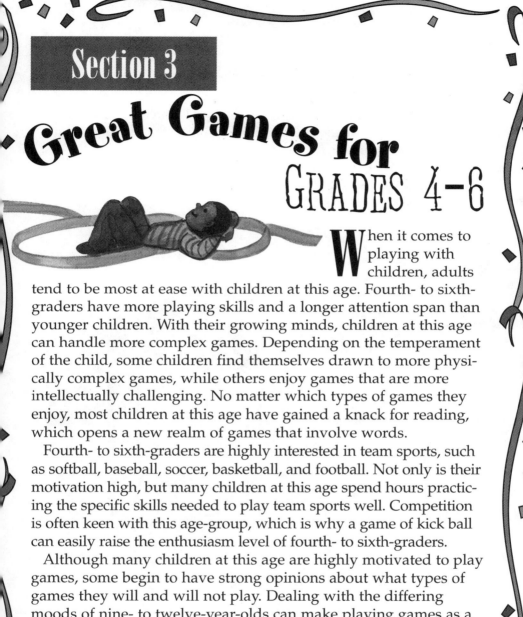

Section 3

Great Games for GRADES 4-6

When it comes to playing with children, adults tend to be most at ease with children at this age. Fourth- to sixth-graders have more playing skills and a longer attention span than younger children. With their growing minds, children at this age can handle more complex games. Depending on the temperament of the child, some children find themselves drawn to more physically complex games, while others enjoy games that are more intellectually challenging. No matter which types of games they enjoy, most children at this age have gained a knack for reading, which opens a new realm of games that involve words.

Fourth- to sixth-graders are highly interested in team sports, such as softball, baseball, soccer, basketball, and football. Not only is their motivation high, but many children at this age spend hours practicing the specific skills needed to play team sports well. Competition is often keen with this age-group, which is why a game of kick ball can easily raise the enthusiasm level of fourth- to sixth-graders.

Although many children at this age are highly motivated to play games, some begin to have strong opinions about what types of games they will and will not play. Dealing with the differing moods of nine- to twelve-year-olds can make playing games as a group a bit tricky. Some want to play the same game again and again. Others, however, get bored and will want to sit out the active playtime. An important key to remember is not to push, but to *invite* children to play. Sometimes a small group of children can get a lot out of just watching a game and cheering on those who are playing. Respecting children's wishes goes a long way when we can do so in ways that also help them feel included.

Jacob's Home Run

Scripture: The story of Jacob's ladder (Genesis 28:10-22)

This Game Teaches: God spoke to Jacob through a dream. God still speaks to us—through the Bible and through other Christians.

Materials: Two Bibles; twenty index cards; two pens; four paper plates

• • • • • • • • • • • • • • • • • •

51

Game: Form two teams. Give each team a Bible, ten index cards, and a pen. Say: **"Open your Bibles to Genesis 28:10-22. As a team, read the story. Then create ten questions from the story to stump the other team. Write one question on one side of the index card and the answer on the back side of the card. Do this for ten different questions."** As the teams prepare, set up a baseball diamond with four paper plates. Each plate represents a base. (For example: first, second, third, and home plate.) After the teams finish, have everyone put away their Bibles. As one team is at bat, the other team will take positions out around the newly created playing field. The pitcher should hold the ten cards.

Have one child from the batting team step up to home plate. The child gets one chance to answer the question correctly. If the child does so, he or she moves to first base. Each time a child on the batting team answers a question correctly, as in a baseball game, he or she moves to first base, and the previous child moves to the next base until reaching home plate and scoring a run. If a child answers incorrectly, the batting team gets one out and another child comes up to bat. When there are three outs, the teams switch positions.

Tally up the score after each team has had the chance to ask each of the ten questions.

After the game ends, say: **"Jacob slept on the ground with a stone as a pillow and had a dream. The dream was of a stairway reaching to heaven with angels going up and down. God spoke to Jacob through a dream. God told Jacob that the land on which he was sleeping would be for Jacob and his children. When Jacob woke up, he poured oil on the pillow because it was sacred. He then named the place Bethel since the word meant it was the house of God."**

Say: **"God still speaks to us. But how?"** Give children the chance to respond. Say: **"God speaks to us through the Bible, through other Christians, and through worship services."**

The Mixed-Up Prodigal Son

Scripture: The prodigal son (Luke 15:11-24)
This Game Teaches: God is a forgiving God.
Materials: Thirteen balloons; an 8½-x-11-inch piece of paper; pen; scissors; Bible

• • • • • • • • • • • • • • • • •

52

Game: Prior to playing the game, fold the piece of paper in half. Then fold the paper like a fan with seven ridges. Open the paper, and you should have fourteen places (marked by the folds in the paper) in which to write. Write one of the bulleted statements below in each of the folded places. (There will be one empty space when you're finished.) Cut the statements apart, and discard the empty space. Place one statement inside each balloon and inflate the balloons.

- A man had two sons.
- The younger son wanted his inheritance.
- The man gave both sons their inheritance.
- The young son left home.
- The young son spent all his inheritance.
- A severe famine hit the land.
- The young son had no way to earn any money and was left penniless.
- He found a job feeding pigs.
- He went back to his father, intending to apologize and beg for a job as a hired worker.
- The father saw the son return and ran to him and kissed him.
- The young son apologized.
- The father threw a huge party to welcome the young son home.
- The father said, "For this son of mine was dead, but now he is alive; he was lost, but now he has been found" (Luke 15:24 TEV).

Have children form a circle. Explain that you want them to bat the balloons around. When you yell, **"Stop and pop!"** children should grab a balloon, pop it, and retrieve the piece of paper inside. (Children can help each other if you have more than thirteen children, or they can pop more than one balloon if you have fewer than thirteen.)

After all the balloons have been popped, have the children put the parable in the correct sequence without looking at the Bible. Then ask someone to read aloud Luke 15:11-24. If the sequence is correct, affirm the children. If the sequence is not correct, encourage the children to rearrange the slips until the story events are in order.

After the game say: **"This is an important parable in the New Testament. The young son apologized to his father for making a poor choice and spending all the money. His father forgave him. Likewise, our God is a forgiving God."**

A Rock and a Stick

Scripture: God tells Moses how to get water from a rock (Numbers 20:1-13)

This Game Teaches: We need to believe in God—even when life gets hard.

Materials: A rock; a small stick (such as an ice cream stick); a well-sealed plastic bottle filled with water

• • • • • • • • • • • • • • • • •

53

Game: Have the children sit in a circle, and place the bottle filled with water in the middle of the group. Designate an area in the room as the doubter's corner.

Say: **"Numbers 20 tells the story of God's people being thirsty and not believing that God would help them. God told Moses to hit a rock twice, and water came flowing out of it. To play this game, we're going to pass around a rock and a stick. When you receive the rock and stick, you are to hit the rock anywhere from one to four times. If you hit the rock twice, which is what Moses did, the first child to grab the bottle of water becomes the new Moses and gets to start the game again. If you grab the bottle when the rock has been hit one, three, or four times, you have to leave the circle and go to the doubter's corner. You aren't allowed back into the game until someone else replaces you in the corner. Any questions?"** Begin by giving one of the children the rock and stick. Say that the child is Moses.

After the game ends, say: **"During this time in the Bible, the Israelites were getting discouraged. Life had become hard again, and so they were having doubts. Even Moses had doubts. But no matter how hard life gets, God is always with us and we need to keep believing."**

It's Impossible!

Scripture: God calls Moses in a burning bush (Exodus 3:1-12)
This Game Teaches: Even Moses had doubts, but nothing is impossible.
Materials: A paper lunch bag; a pair of mittens; a piece of string; a shelled peanut for each child (Have some sealed hard candy available for children with peanut allergies.)

• • • • • • • • • • • • • • • • •

Game: Prior to the game prepare a lunch bag with a shelled peanut inside for each child. Tie each bag with a piece of string. (Create one or two bags with hard candy inside as a peanut alternative.) Give each child a pair of mittens and a sealed bag.

Say: **"When I tell you to begin, put on your mittens. Then untie the string with only your mitten-covered hands. Open the bag. Take out what's inside and eat it, taking off the covering with your mitten-covered hands. When you finish, tie up the bag with your mitten-covered hands."**

Begin the activity. Monitor children's frustration, since some may get extremely frustrated by this game. Encourage children to go more slowly and take their time. After the game ends, say: **"God appeared to Moses in a burning bush. He wanted Moses to lead God's people. What did Moses say? Moses thought it was impossible—just as many of you thought it was impossible to do things with the mittens on. But nothing is impossible. Sometimes life can get hard and frustrating, but if we take our time and have faith, we can do anything."**

Bible Verse Spelling

Scripture: Short verses, such as John 11:35: "Jesus wept";
  1 Thessalonians 5:16: "Be joyful always"; 1 Thessalonians
  5:17: "Pray at all times"; and Psalm 150:6a: "Praise the LORD"
  (TEV)

This Game Teaches: When we study God's Word, we can
  learn more about our world and how to act in meaningful
  ways.

Materials: Two pieces of clothesline at least 6 feet long; 40
  clothespins; 4 chairs; 58 pieces of 8½-x-11-inch paper; markers

• • • • • • • • • • • • • • • • •

55

Game: Form two teams, and give each team 20 clothespins, 29
pieces of 8½-x-11-inch paper, and markers. Have each team write
the letters of the alphabet on the paper, writing one letter on each
piece of paper about the size of the paper. As teams work, set up
two chairs next to one team so that they face the other team.
Place them about five feet apart and run the clothesline between the
two chairs. Create the same setup with the other two chairs and
clothesline next to the other team.

After the teams finish, have each team create one additional page
for each of the following letters: "a," "l," and "s."

Then say: **"We're going to play a cooperative Bible Verse Spelling
game. I'll give you a Bible verse, and I'll signal which team will
create the first word and which team will create the second word.
Find the letters for the word you're creating and hang them on the
clothesline facing the other team, using two clothespins to hold up
each letter."**

Use scriptures that have short verses, such as John 11:35: "Jesus
wept"; 1 Thessalonians 5:16: "Be joyful always"; 1 Thessalonians 5:17:
"Pray at all times"; and Psalm 150:6a: "Praise the LORD" (TEV).

For example, for John 11:35 one team will spell the word "Jesus,"
and the other team will spell the word "wept." For 1 Thessalonians
5:17, have one team create the word "pray" and the other team create
the word "at" before having the first team spell the word "all" and
the other team spell the word "times."

After the game ends, say: **"The Bible is full of helpful words that
tell us how to act as Christians. When we study God's Word, we can
learn more about our world and how to act in meaningful ways."**

Where's Adam?
Where's Eve?

Scripture: Adam and Eve hide from God (Genesis 3:8-10)
This Game Teaches: God always loves and accepts us and
  wants us to tell the truth.
Materials: None

• • • • • • • • • • • • • • • • •

Game: Ask for a volunteer. Call her or him "God," and have
the person leave the room.

Ask for two other volunteers. Call one "Adam" and the
other "Eve." Have everyone stand and spread out around the
room. Have Adam and Eve separate and mix in with the rest
of the children.

Bring the child waiting outside the room back in. Say: **"This
child, the one we've called 'God,' will try to pick out Adam and
Eve. God will walk around while everyone else moves around
the room. When God gets close to either Adam or Eve, everyone
is to clap loudly. When God moves away from Adam or Eve,
clap more quietly. Stop clapping if God moves too far away
from Adam or Eve. After Adam and Eve are found, the game
ends."**

Play the game. Sometimes children will want to play it more
than once so that others have a chance to be God, Adam, or Eve.

Afterward say: **"When we do
something we're not sup-
posed to do, like Adam
and Eve eating the apple,
we often want to hide.
But no matter what we
do, it's important to admit
what we've done. God
always loves us and
always accepts us and
wants us to tell the truth."**

Spread the Good News

Scripture: The Great Commission (Matthew 28:18-20)
This Game Teaches: It's important to spread the good news.
Materials: A flying saucer for each group of four children; a
large playing area such as a gym or outdoor area

• • • • • • • • • • • • • • • • • •

57

Game: Form groups of four, and give each group a flying
saucer. Have each group stand in a single line, with each
child about three feet apart from the next person in line.

Say: **"When I say 'Begin,' the first person in each group
will throw the flying saucer to the next person in line. As
soon as you throw the saucer, run to the end of your team line
so that you can play again. Once you catch the saucer, throw it
to the next person. Whenever you throw the flying saucer, say,
'It's good news. God is always with us.' When your team reaches
the end of the play area, then work backward to the beginning.
Any questions?"**

Begin the activity. After the game ends, say: **"In Matthew 28,
Jesus came back and commanded the disciples to go to people
everywhere and tell them the good news. That means spreading
out. That means telling the good news. That means sticking
with it, even if it isn't going well."**

Poor Job

Scripture: The story of the plight of Job (Job 1–2, 42)

This Game Teaches: Bad things happen, and bad things become worse when people are hurtful instead of helpful.

Materials: Four paintbrushes and face paint; several stuffed animals; an index card with Job 42:2 written on it: "I know, LORD, that you are all-powerful; that you can do everything you want." (TEV)

• • • • • • • • • • • • • • • • •

Game: Ask for a volunteer who doesn't mind having her or his face painted. Tell the group that this person is Job, and have her or him sit in front of the group. Ask for four more volunteers. Give each a paintbrush and a small amount of face paint. Explain that these people will be painting sores all over Job's skin. Have the other children surround Job with stuffed animals. Next, invite everyone to talk about how good life is.

Ask the children without the paintbrushes to gradually remove the stuffed animals until they're gone, and then sit and watch. Ask the painters to come and paint dots all over Job's skin. When they finish, ask them to sit with the rest of the group.

Whisper to one of the children to go over to Job and ask these two questions repeatedly while walking around her or him: "What's the matter with you? What happened to all your stuff?" Then whisper to another child to go to Job and repeat the following statement while walking around Job: "You must have been bad, bad, bad." Whisper to a third child to go to Job and say these two sentences over and over: "Don't believe in God. God isn't helping you."

Give the index card to Job. Whisper in his ear to stand up and shout: "Stop! Sit down!" to the three children walking around him, chanting. Then ask Job to read the scripture aloud.

After the game ends, say: **"Bad things happen, and we don't like it when they do. But God doesn't cause bad things to happen. God is always with us—even when we are absolutely miserable. What we need to do when people are going through hard times is not to blame them and not to tell them to stop believing in God as these three so-called friends did. We can be there for people and comfort them in their hard times."**

Body Scramble

Scripture: The star in the sky (Matthew 2:2); the five loaves and two fish (Matthew 14:13-21); the Sermon on the Mount (Matthew 5:1); healing the sick and lame (Matthew 8:28-34); and Jesus' baptism (Matthew 3:17)

This Game Teaches: The stories of Jesus help us to become better people.

Materials: An 8½-x-11-inch piece of paper for each child; markers; masking tape; a Bible

• • • • • • • • • • • • • • • • • •

59

Game: Count the number of children present. If six are present, have each write one of these letters in large print on a piece of 8½-x-11-inch paper: "a," "n," "o," "r," "s," and "t." If there are more than six children, assign the same letter to more than one person. For twelve or more children, form two teams with each team having its own set of letters.

Have children tape their letter to the front of their chests. Say: **"We're going to talk about Jesus' life. I'll start out with a well-known story, and I want you to identify the missing word. Don't shout out the word. Instead, get together as a group, whisper instructions, and spell the word by standing side by side in the correct order of the letters. For example, let's say the missing word was 'rat.' What would you do?"** Have children create the

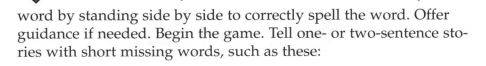

word by standing side by side to correctly spell the word. Offer guidance if needed. Begin the game. Tell one- or two-sentence stories with short missing words, such as these:

- The wise men saw a _____ in the sky (*star*—Matthew 2:2).
- The people _____ the five loaves and two fish (*ate*—Matthew 14:13-21).
- When Jesus gave the Sermon on the Mount, he _____ on a hill (*sat*—Matthew 5:1).
- When Jesus healed the sick and those who couldn't walk, the people who were healed usually _____ to tell others what had happened (*ran*—Matthew 8:28-34).
- When Jesus was baptized, a voice came from the heavens and said, "This is my own dear _____, with whom I am pleased" (*Son*—Matthew 3:17 TEV).

After the game say: **"We can learn a lot about what Jesus did by studying the stories about him. In one story people who couldn't walk for years ran after Jesus healed them. They were excited. They couldn't wait to tell everyone the good news. The stories of Jesus help us to become better people."**

The Israelites:
The Winners

Scripture: Israel defeats the Midianites (Judges 8)
This Game Teaches: When God's people followed God, God
helped them. When we stay close to God, we can do
incredible things.
Materials: Three soft, large balls (such as foam balls); a gym-
nasium or large outdoor play area

• • • • • • • • • • • • • • • •

60

Game: Designate a play area so that everyone knows what's
in bounds and what's out of bounds. Ask for three volunteers. Give each a soft, large ball. Explain that they represent
God's people—the Israelites—and that they are being led in a
war against the Midianites. Tell the rest of the children that
they are the Midianites, the bad guys. The children representing
the Midianites are to laugh at the three Israelites for having such a
small team.

Say: **"The Midianites are to start running after the Israelites to
defeat them, but as soon as the Israelites start throwing the
balls, the Midianites will turn around and run away from the
Israelites. If someone from the Midianite team gets hit with the
ball, he or she must fall to the ground and stay there for the rest
of the game. The Israelites can run and get the ball once it has
been thrown and throw the ball again. Let's play until only the
three Israelites are left standing."**

After the game ends, say: **"Gideon was one of the Israelites,
and he didn't believe that he could lead the Israelites to defeat
the Midianites. In Judges 6:15, Gideon said, 'But Lord, how can
I rescue Israel? My clan is the weakest in the tribe of Manasseh,
and I am the least important member of my family' (TEV). Even
though Gideon never thought he could win, God helped him
defeat the Midianites. So, when we stay close to God, we, too,
can do incredible things that we never thought we'd be able to
do."**

Leapin' Lazarus

Scripture: Lazarus rises from the dead (John 11:38-44)
This Game Teaches: Jesus had an incredible power to heal.
  We follow a powerful God.
Materials: A pile of stones for each group of four children; a
  large playing area, such as a gym or outdoor area

Game: Go to a large playing area. Form groups of
four with children standing
in a single line. Have the
first person in each group
take twelve large steps forward
and then lie on the ground. The
second person will take eight
large steps forward and lie on the ground. The third person will
take four large steps forward and lie on the ground. Give a pile of
rocks to the fourth child. Have the child put the rocks in front of
the person closest to her or him and then move backward four
large steps.

Say: **"We're going to play a game about Jesus raising a man
named Lazarus from the dead. When I say to begin, the child
who is standing runs to the pile of rocks and picks them up and
carries them to the place where the next-closest child is lying.
This may take a couple of trips or just one. Once all the rocks
are moved, the child runs back to where the first child was
lying, touches the child's face, and says, 'Lazarus, come out!'
The lying child leaps up and runs with the first child to the pile
of rocks and repeats the process with the next child lying down.
As each Lazarus is healed, there are more children to help move
the rocks."**

Play the game. Afterward say: **"Lazarus had been buried for four
days when Jesus came along. No one believed that Lazarus could
live again. But Jesus had an incredible power to heal. Not only
did he make the blind see and the lame walk, but he sometimes
even brought the dead back to life. We follow a powerful God."**

61

Building the Tower of Babel

Scripture: The Tower of Babel (Genesis 11)

This Game Teaches: Building is easier when you can talk and work together, unlike what happened in the story of Babel.

Materials: Lots of clothespins

· · · · · · · · · · · · · · · · ·

62

Game: Form two teams, and give each team a large supply of clothespins. Say: **"The goal of this game is to create a tower out of the clothespins. Make a tower as tall as you can. However, there is one hitch. This group** (point to a group) **can talk and work together as best as they can. This other group** (point to the other group) **cannot speak to each other or even use hand gestures. Any questions?"**

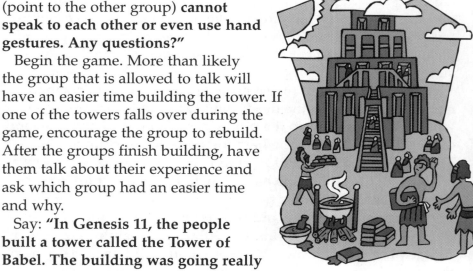

Begin the game. More than likely the group that is allowed to talk will have an easier time building the tower. If one of the towers falls over during the game, encourage the group to rebuild. After the groups finish building, have them talk about their experience and ask which group had an easier time and why.

Say: **"In Genesis 11, the people built a tower called the Tower of Babel. The building was going really well until the people started making bad choices and not following God. Soon, everyone was speaking a different language. No one could understand anyone else. The building stopped because everyone was confused, and it was hard to work together. We saw this when our two groups built their own towers. It's easier to accomplish a goal when we can talk and work together."**

The Trusty Trio

Scripture: The Trinity of God, Jesus, and the Holy Spirit (2 Corinthians 13:13)

This Game Teaches: The more we learn about each member of the Trinity, the better we can understand who we worship.

Materials: Nine pieces of 8½-x-11-inch paper; markers; two rolls of masking tape; two dictionaries

• • • • • • • • • • • • • • • • •

Game: Before the game, create three signs out of three pieces of the paper, labeling one "God," another "Jesus," and the last "Holy Spirit." Attach the "God" paper to one wall (such as the east wall), the "Jesus" paper to the opposite wall (the west wall), and the "Holy Spirit" to one of the other empty walls (north or south wall) with masking tape. On two of the remaining sheets of paper write the word "God" vertically. (The children will be creating acrostics with this.) Do the same with the words "Jesus" and "Holy Spirit," making two sheets for each word.

Create two teams. Give each team three pieces of paper (each piece listing a different name of the Trinity), a roll of masking tape, and a dictionary. Say: **"We're going to have a race. As a team, your job is to write a word for each letter that describes the person. For example, you could use the word 'Good' for the letter 'G' in the word 'God,' before going on to the letter 'O.' After your team finishes a word, take a piece of masking tape and run to the 'God' wall and tape your team's creation near it. Then work on the letters in the other two words. The team to finish first is the winner, but choose words carefully. Use your dictionaries for help."**

When the teams finish, have them read their creations aloud. In some instances, some letters will be insightful, and others silly.

After the game, say: **"We believe that we worship a God who is the unity of three persons: Father, Son, and Holy Spirit. We also use the word 'God' for the Father and 'Jesus' for the Son. The more we can learn about attributes and characteristics of these three, the better we can understand who we worship and go to in prayer."**

Jacob or Esau

Scripture: The blessing by Isaac (Genesis 27:1-29)

This Game Teaches: Although Esau was supposed to get the birthright, Jacob got it instead. It's much better to be honest.

Materials: Blindfold; three patches of brown fake fur (from a fabric store); tape; two safety pins; two stuffed animals; scissors

. . . .

64

Game: Cut one of the patches of fur in half so that each patch can be taped to a child's hand. As a class, study this story before playing the game to familiarize the children with the events. Ask for four volunteers. Have one child be Jacob. Blindfold another child, who will be Isaac. Pin a patch of fur to the chest of another child, and call him Esau. Give Esau a stuffed animal to hold. Give the other stuffed animal, the remaining fur, tape, and safety pin to the child who will be Rebekah. Have Rebekah hold these items behind her back. (During the game Rebekah will help pin the large piece of fur to Jacob's chest, and then tape the other two pieces of fur onto Jacob's hands.) Ask the rest of the children to sit and watch.

Have the four children reenact the story, with Esau going out to the field and "hanging out" with one stuffed animal. Rebekah then encourages Jacob to put on the fur, take the stuffed animal, and pretend to be Esau. Next, Jacob presents the stuffed animal to Isaac and receives the blessing. Encourage the volunteers to "ham up" their parts in the story.

Afterward say: **"Esau was supposed to get the birthright because he was the firstborn. Isaac, who was blind, was tricked and instead gave the birthright to Jacob. Later in the Bible we read about Esau's anger with Jacob for stealing his birthright, but there is no mention of Rebekah's part in the trick. Both Jacob and Rebekah were wrong. It's much better to be honest and to receive things fairly."**

Mirror, Mirror

Scripture: The faith of Bible heroes (Hebrews 11)
This Game Teaches: We can be like the heroes of the Bible.
Materials: Bibles; a mirror

• • • • • • • • • • • • • • • • •

Game: Have children read Hebrews 11. Ask them to select one of the Bible heroes mentioned (such as Abel, Enoch, Noah, Abraham, Isaac, Jacob, Joseph, Moses' parents, Moses, and the Israelite) who they most want to be like. Next have them sit in a circle. Give one person a mirror and have her or him stand up, look in the mirror, and say the name of their Bible hero and what he or she admires about the person. As each child finishes, he or she gives the mirror to another child. Play until everyone has had a turn.

After the game say: **"There are many admirable people in the Bible. We can learn many things from them—how to act, what to believe, how to talk. Every time you look in the mirror, remember your Bible hero and think of ways you can be more like her or him."**

65

Warning Shots

Scripture: Jonathan warns David about Saul (1 Samuel 20)
This Game Teaches: David was saved because Jonathan warned him when his life was in danger. Good friends like Jonathan help us when we need it.
Materials: An ice cream stick for each child; an area that has room for children to throw

. . . .

66

Game: Give each child an ice cream stick and say: **"In 1 Samuel, David's life was in danger by King Saul. Now King Saul had a son, Jonathan, who loved David and wanted to keep David safe. Jonathan urged David to hide in the wilderness, and then Jonathan fired arrows into the wilderness to signal to David when his life was in danger. Now it's our turn to be Jonathan. Let's line up and throw our ice cream sticks as far as we can, as warning shots."**

Have the children throw their ice cream sticks. Encourage them to run out and pick up a stick and return. Say: **"David's life is in danger, and he needs another signal to tell him to stay in the wilderness."** Have the children throw the sticks again. Do this a number of times.

Afterward say: **"Because Jonathan fired arrows into the wilderness, David knew that he needed to stay in hiding. After a while King Saul became less angry, and David was able to come out. It's good to have friends like Jonathan who are willing to help us out when we are in danger."**

Hidden Disciples

Scripture: The twelve disciples (Matthew 10:2-4)

This Game Teaches: The twelve disciples teach us about following God.

Materials: Twelve index cards; marker; alphabet letters (for example, magnetic letters, dry alphabet macaroni, alphabet flash cards, or other types of letters of the alphabet—be sure you have lots of letters)

• • • • • • • • • • • • • • • • •

67

Game: Before the game, use a marker to write the name of each disciple on a separate index card. The names, according to Matthew 10:2-4, are Peter, Andrew, John, James, Philip, Bartholomew, Thomas, Matthew, James (yes, a second one), Thaddaeus, Simon, and Judas.

Have the children gather together, and pour the letters in front of them. Say: **"The twelve disciples are hidden in here. With someone near you, take an index card and look for the letters to spell the name of the disciple named on the card. When you finish, take another index card and spell the name of that disciple. Keep the spellings you create."**

As the children work, remind them that this is not a race but instead a puzzle to find all twelve disciples. After all twelve are found, talk about the names. Ask if anyone has the same name of one of the disciples, or if they know of someone with the same name.

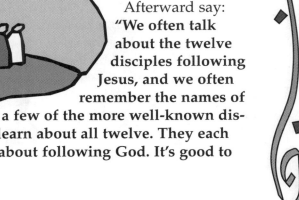

Afterward say: **"We often talk about the twelve disciples following Jesus, and we often remember the names of a few of the more well-known disciples, but it's important to learn about all twelve. They each have something to teach us about following God. It's good to follow God."**

Water at the Well

Scripture: Isaac meeting Rebekah at the well (Genesis 24)
This Game Teaches: We need water to live. In Bible times,
  people like Rebekah had to get water from a well.
Materials: A hot day; paper cups; buckets of water equal to
  the number of teams you create and the same number of
  empty buckets

. . . .

68

Game: Form two to four teams depending on the size of
your group. Have the teams line up behind one another. Give
each team an empty bucket by placing it next to the first person in line. Place a bucket of water about ten feet in front of
each line. Give the first child in each line an empty paper cup.
Say: **"In Bible times, you had to walk to the well to get
water. Then you had to carry the water home. This took a lot of
time. When I say, 'Go,' I want you to run to the bucket of water
in front of you, fill the cup with water, place it on your head,
and walk back slowly to the next person in line. When you get
there, pour the water carefully into your team's empty bucket.
Then hand off the cup to the next person, who will repeat the
activity. Ready? Let's go."**

This game is a big hit on hot days, especially if your church
doesn't have air-conditioning. Be sensitive to children who may
not want to get wet. (Encourage them to
hold the cup with both hands while
they walk back slowly.)

After the game ends, say: **"Isaac
met Rebekah at the well, and she
gave Isaac and his camels water.
We need water to live. Imagine
what our lives would be like if
we had to go to a well every
day to get water as Rebekah
had to do."**

Hide and Sneak

Scripture: Rahab and the spies (Joshua 2)
This Game Teaches: People can help others.
Materials: An outdoor or indoor area with lots of places to hide; several blankets

. . . .

Game: Ask for five volunteers. Instruct the other children to leave the area while you explain the game. Have two of the volunteers play spies from the Israelites. Another child can be Rahab, while the remaining two can be people who live in Jericho. Explain that the spies are the good guys. When asked by the bad-guy officers, Rahab and the two people from Jericho are to say that no one is in their homes. After the bad-guy officers leave, the two spies are to come out and sneak away. Tell the spies to hide. Have Rahab use the blankets to cover them up completely.

Explain to the rest of the children that they are the bad-guy officers and they are looking for spies. Their job is to ask people if anyone is in their homes. Then they are to search around, but they are not allowed to lift up any tablecloths, blankets, or other coverings.

Give the bad-guy officers time to look. Signal them to stop and give the two spies time to escape. Then bring everyone together and ask these questions:

• Rahab, how did it feel to hide spies?
• Spies, what were you thinking when you heard the bad-guy officers nearby?
• Bad-guy officers, how did you feel when you didn't find anybody?
• Why do you think this is a story in the Bible?

After the game ends, say: **"As people of God, we need other people to help us at times. That's what Rahab did for the two spies. Rahab was not an Israelite like the two spies. In fact, many people thought she was a bad person. But Rahab helped the two spies and kept them safe. As Christians, we must always be ready to do good things and to help good people."**

It All Adds Up

Scripture: Growing in Christ (Ephesians 4:1-32)
This Game Teaches: Each small action we do adds up.
Materials: A piece of tape; a Bible; a ball of yarn; a pair of
scissors; a table or chair

• • • • • • • • • • • • • • • •

70

Game: Before you play the game, cut a piece of yarn and
tape it to a chalkboard, door, or wall at about eye level for the
children. Have the children form a single-file line. Set the
table or chair near the first person in line. Set the ball of yarn
and scissors on it. Open the Bible to Ephesians 4, and set it
near the yarn and scissors.

Say: **"When I say to begin, the first person in line will cut a
piece of yarn from the ball. Then he or she will start reading
Ephesians 4 aloud until he or she gets to a spot that gives advice
on how to live as a Christian. At that point, stop reading. Reread
the advice aloud again, and then run up to the yarn that is taped
to the wall. Tie your piece onto it. Meanwhile, while the first
child is doing this, the second child should look at Ephesians 4
and find the place where the first child stopped. Then begin
reading at the spot when the first child returns to the end of the
line. The activity then repeats for each person in line. We'll
keep doing this activity until we finish reading all of
Ephesians 4."**

Start the game. You may need to help children keep track of
where the reading stops, particularly children who may have
reading challenges. When the group gets
through the entire chapter, stop the game.
Show the children the long chain of yarn.
After the game ends, say: **"Ephesians
4 is full of good advice on how to act
as a Christian. Every day, we need to
act in these ways. Each act may seem
small, but the more acts we do, the
more they add up and make
a big difference."**

Haircut Horror

Scripture: Samson and Delilah (Judges 16)
This Game Teaches: Delilah learned Samson's secret of strength, cut his hair, and made him weak. It's important to watch out for tricky people who could hurt us.
Materials: A wig (preferably with long hair)

• • • • • • • • • • • • • • • • •

Game: Ask for a volunteer to be Samson, and put a wig on that person's head. Say: **"Samson is in a tricky position. He needs to guard his hair while also trying to tag the rest of you so that you cannot get his hair. Everyone else is going to be Delilah. Your goal is to try to get the wig without being tagged by Samson first. If you're tagged, you must freeze in position, and you cannot try to get the wig for the rest of the game."**

Let the children play the game. If the wig comes off too quickly, play again and enlist a partner for Samson who can help guard his hair and also tag people.

After the game ends, say: **"Samson was the strongest man alive, and Samson loved Delilah. Delilah wanted money, and the Philistines (the bad guys that wanted to stop Samson) told Delilah if they could find out the secret to Samson's strength, they would each pay her 1,100 pieces of silver. This was like becoming a millionaire. Delilah was greedy, and she worked until she finally got Samson to tell his secret. She cut Samson's hair, and he lost his strength and was taken prisoner. Samson would have been better off without Delilah. It's important to watch out for tricky people who could hurt us."**

Wise Words

Scripture: The words of Jesus (the Gospels: Matthew, Mark, Luke, John)

This Game Teaches: The Gospels are full of words of wisdom about how to live as Christians.

Materials: A large number of index cards; a pen or pencil for each child; two containers (such as baskets, buckets, or boxes)

• • • • • • • • • • • • • • • • •

72

Game: Form two teams, and give each a stack of index cards. Hand each child a pen or pencil. Place an empty container about ten feet from each group.

Say: **"We've been learning about what it means to be a Christian. Throughout Jesus' life, in the books of Matthew, Mark, Luke, and John, Jesus told us a lot about how to act. When I say to begin, I want each of you to write something you've learned that Jesus said. It doesn't have to be a Bible verse, although it can be. It just needs to be something you've learned about how to be a Christian. When you finish writing, run to the container and drop your card in. Run back to your group and write something else. Drop this card in the container also. Continue to do this until I say to stop. Any questions?"**

Start the game. Afterward, instead of counting the number of cards in each container, pull out the cards and read them aloud. Comment on what the children are learning.

Say: **"Loving our neighbors. Loving ourselves. Praying. Following God. All of these are great examples of how to be a Christian. The Gospels are full of words of wisdom."**

Using Your Head

Scripture: Solomon's wisdom (1 Kings 3:5-9)
This Game Teaches: Being wise takes practice.
Materials: Ten children; one 8½-x-11-inch piece of paper for
each child; masking tape; markers; a coin

● ● ● ● ● ● ● ● ● ● ● ● ● ● ● ● ● ●

73

Game: Create two groups. Give each group markers and each child a piece of paper. Ask the children of one group to make a large letter "O" on their papers. Ask the children in the other group to make a large letter "X" on their papers. Draw a tic-tac-toe framework on an indoor surface with masking tape. (On a warm day, do this activity by drawing the tic-tac-toe framework on a sidewalk or pavement with chalk.)

Say: **"In the Bible, Solomon was known for being wise. In other words, he used his head and made a lot of smart choices. Now, let's play a game where we have to think and use our heads. We're going to play human tic-tac-toe. I'll flip a coin to see which team goes first. Each team will then take turns having a child take a place in the tic-tac-toe framework. As a team, work together to figure out your strategy for winning."**

Practice playing the game a few times. Encourage the teams to give each member a chance to play, so that if someone didn't play in the first game, they get to start the next game.

After the game say: **"Although Solomon prayed for wisdom and was given wisdom by God, Solomon had to keep using his wisdom and keep trying—just as we did in tic-tac-toe. We don't always win when we use our heads, but we always can learn and improve."**

Hop to It!

Scripture: The life of Jesus (the Gospel of Luke: 2:15-16, 42; 3:22; 4:1-12; 5:8-10, 12-14; 6:12-16; 8:4, 19-20; 10:38-39; 19:1-19; 22:48, 54-62; 23:26; 24:7)

This Game Teaches: When we learn about Jesus, we learn about what it means to be a Christian.

Materials: Sidewalk or outdoor pavement; a piece of chalk for each child; a Bible; a timer (optional)

• • • • • • • • • • • • • • • • • •

74

Game: On a warm day, find a place outside where the children can create a hopscotch outline on the sidewalk or pavement. Give each child a piece of chalk. Open the Bible to the book of Luke.

Say: **"I'm going to ask questions about Jesus' life. If you know the answer, shout it out. If you're correct, I'll say 'yes' and then take your chalk and draw a square with a number in it. This is a cooperative game, which means we will all be working on the same hopscotch shape. So the first person with the correct answer will draw the first box and put a number one in it. The second person will draw a second box with the number two in it above the first box. When ten boxes are drawn, yell out 'winner!' Then everyone will take a turn to celebrate by hopping on the winning shape. Any questions?"**

Begin asking questions. After the children

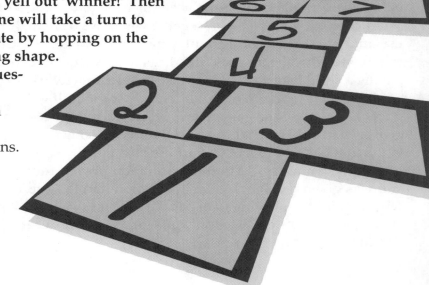

finish, have them each hop through the shape. If you want to repeat the game, use a timer and encourage the group to better its own record.

Here are a few sample questions:

- Where was Jesus born? (*Bethlehem*—Luke 2:15-16)
- How old was Jesus when his parents lost him at the temple? (*Twelve*—Luke 2:42)
- What appeared when Jesus was baptized? (*A dove*—Luke 3:22)
- What was one of the three temptations? (*Turn stone to bread; Bow down and I'll give you the kingdoms of the world; Throw yourself down from the highest point*—Luke 4:1-12)
- Can you name one of the first disciples? (*Simon Peter*—Luke 5:8; *James and John*—Luke 5:10)
- What disease did Jesus heal that created sores all over a person's body? (*Leprosy*—Luke 5:12-14)
- How many disciples followed Jesus? (*Twelve*—Luke 6:12-16)
- Jesus told a special kind of story. What was it called? (*Parable*—Luke 8:4)
- Did Jesus have any sisters? (*No*—Luke 8:19-20)
- What were the names of the two women who Jesus visited at their house? (*Martha and Mary*—Luke 10:38-39)
- What was the name of the short tax collector who climbed a tree? (*Zacchaeus*—Luke 19:1-19)
- Which disciple kissed Jesus so that Jesus would be arrested? (*Judas*—Luke 22:48)
- Which disciple pretended not to know Jesus? (*Peter*—Luke 22:54-62)
- What did Jesus die on? (*A cross*—Luke 23:26)
- How many days after he died did Jesus rise from the dead? (*Three*—Luke 24:7)

After the game say: **"The events of Jesus' life are important to know. When we learn about Jesus, we learn about what it means to be a Christian. By following Jesus' example and doing what Jesus said, we can be better people who make a better world."**

Pictures of Creation

Scripture: The Creation story (Genesis 1–2:4)

This Game Teaches: God created the world in seven days, and, like God, we need both work and rest.

Materials: Various old magazines; scissors; two pieces of poster board; masking tape; two tape dispensers; a list of the seven days of creation printed on a chalkboard or newsprint

• • • • • • • • • • • • • • • • • •

75

Game: Form two groups. Hang a piece of poster board about ten feet away from each group. Give each group a stack of old magazines, scissors, and a tape dispenser. Write the following list on a chalkboard or newsprint:

Day 1—Night and day

Day 2—Sky and water

Day 3—Land and plants

Day 4—Sun, moon, and stars

Day 5—Sea creatures and birds

Day 6—Land animals and people

Day 7—Rest

Say: **"When I tell you to begin, start flipping through the magazines, looking for pictures that fit the seven days. When you find one, name it for your group. Tear or cut it out of the magazine, and run to your team's poster board and tape the picture to**

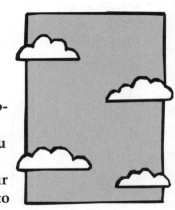

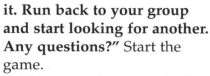

it. **Run back to your group and start looking for another. Any questions?"** Start the game.

After teams have finished, have each group give a pictorial report, showing the magazine pictures they found and how they represent the seven days.

Afterward, say: **"The Creation story is the first story in the Bible, and it's an important one, but we often forget what God created on what day. We also tend to forget about resting after we've done a lot of work. We need both—work and rest."**

Great Games for
MIXED GRADES (GRADES K-6)

Finding games that will interest a wide age range of children isn't easy, particularly if you have lots of young children (such as five-year-olds) and older children (such as twelve-year-olds). The differences between a five-year-old and a twelve-year-old often can feel as vast as those between an infant and a pre-schooler. Their capabilities are very different.

The trick with playing games with children of different ages is to find games that younger children understand and can participate in meaningfully while not boring the older children. It's this issue that causes most groups including children of different ages to suffer large attendance drops. Often having one or two extra adults (or older teenagers) involved so that you can create programming that allows for children to play games in smaller groups with children close to their own age can help. Also helpful is to have older children do the Bible study that the game is based on before taking charge of games played by the entire group. Older children can also teach and look out for the younger children. Encouraging older children to befriend younger children is an important part of creating intergenerational community in a church, and these friendships also can help children feel more connected to their church.

The essential element for playing games with children of different ages is *fun*. When children laugh and have fun, they forget there are differences between them. When children have been absorbed in play, they leave feeling satisfied, stimulated, and connected.

Pillars of Salt

Scripture: Sodom and Gomorrah (Genesis 18–19)
This Game Teaches: We need to keep trusting God and moving forward, not having doubts and looking back.
Materials: A large indoor or outdoor play area; a whistle

• • • • • • • • • • • • • • • • •

Game: Have children line up along one side of the play area. Say: **"We're going to play a game. When I tell you to begin, walk forward four steps and then turn around and walk backward four steps. Then turn around again and walk forward four steps, and continue to repeat this pattern until you reach the other end of the playing area. Then stop. Whenever I blow the whistle, stop in whatever position you are in. If you are walking backward, you must freeze and stay where you are for the rest of the game. You are frozen in time. If you are walking forward you can move again when I say to go."**

Play the game. Blow the whistle periodically. Watch for children who may try to continue to play even if they're supposed to be frozen. By the end of the game, children should be scattered throughout the play area. Bring the children together and say: **"In the story of Sodom and Gomorrah, God destroyed the cities because they were filled with evil people. But Lot wasn't evil. His family was allowed to flee. However, they were warned not to turn around and look back but to keep moving forward. Lot's wife didn't listen. She turned back, and when she did, she became a pillar of salt. We need to keep trusting God and moving forward, not having doubts and looking back."**

Run, David, Run!

Scripture: Saul hunts for David (1 Samuel 19)
This Game Teaches: It's important to be aware of what's happening around you.
Materials: None

Game: Have children form a circle and sit down. Ask for one volunteer. Say: **"This game is a lot like 'Duck, Duck, Gray Duck.' In 'Duck, Duck, Gray Duck,' a volunteer walks around the outside of the circle and taps each child's head, saying, 'duck.' When the volunteer taps a child's head and says 'gray duck,' the child whose head has been tapped jumps up and runs around the circle, trying to catch the volunteer before he or she runs around the circle and sits in the child's spot. If the child catches the volunteer, the volunteer taps heads again. If the child doesn't catch the volunteer, the child becomes the new volunteer.**

"In this game there are two differences. First, the person tapping children's heads will be known as David. And second, our David will say the word 'careful' each time and then the word 'Saul' when he or she chooses the child who will do the chasing. Otherwise, the game is the same. Any questions?"

Play the game. After the game ends, say: **"We need to stay alert to what's happening around us. That's what David did. David knew that Saul didn't like him and wanted to hurt him. So David was ready. When Saul came after him, David ran. By watching for danger around him, David was able to keep himself safe."**

Your Autograph, Please

Scripture: The world census (Luke 2:1-3)
This Game Teaches: We each count with God.
Materials: A spiral notebook with marker; a jump rope; a
   stuffed rabbit; a chair; a simple puzzle (for children ages 3–6);
   a small rubber ball

• • • • • • • • • • • • • • • • •

Game: Set up six stations with one of the above items at each station. Have children go to the different stations (except for the one with the spiral notebook and marker) so that each station has approximately the same number of children.

Say: **"The reason that Mary and Joseph went to Bethlehem was because everyone had to register for the census in the town in which they were born. Your job is to make the same trek. First, perform the task at your station, then go to another station and do the task there. You must go to and finish the task at all five stations before going to the notebook station. When you get to the notebook station, write your name in the notebook and take a seat until the other children finish. This is not a race. Take your time and make sure you do each thing.**

"Before we begin, let's talk about the task at each station. Remember the number *three.* **That's how many times you have to do each task at each station. At this station** (point to the jump rope), **you are to jump rope three times. At this station** (point to the stuffed rabbit), **you are to pick up and hold the rabbit as you hop three times. At this station** (point to the chair), **you are to sit in the chair and count aloud to three. At this station** (point to the puzzle), **you are to put the puzzle completely together, say 'Wow' three times, and then dump the puzzle. At this station** (point to the ball), **you are to bounce the ball three times. Then go to the notebook and write your name before sitting down."**

Have children play the game. After the game say: **"Every person counts. Although the kings wanted people to be counted so that they could tax them, God keeps track of everyone because God loves each one of us. We each count with God."**

Blow Those Trumpets!

Scripture: The walls of Jericho (Joshua 6:12-20)
This Game Teaches: God keeps God's promises. We can trust God.
Materials: Seven children; a red handkerchief or dishcloth

• • • • • • • • • • • • • • • • •

79

Game: Briefly tell the story of the Battle of Jericho. Emphasize the number *seven:* the seven days of walking around the city walls, seven priests holding trumpets behind the ark, and circling the city seven times on the seventh day.

Ask for one volunteer, and have that person be Rahab. Give Rahab a red handkerchief or dishcloth to hold. Ask for four other volunteers. These four children are the walls of Jericho. Have the four children surround the child representing Rahab with their backs turned toward her or him.

Tell about Rahab helping the Israelites by hiding a couple of them when they came to spy on the city. After she helped them escape death, the Israelites promised that God would keep her and everyone in her house safe. Rahab was told to tie a red cloth to her house as a sign that she would be kept safe.

Ask all the other children to stand. Say: **"Let's march around the walls of Jericho. We have to do this seven times. After the seventh time, act as if you're playing a trumpet and make trumpet noises. Then I'll signal you to stop. Together, we'll shout out 'Fall!' When that happens, the children being the walls of Jericho should fall, but Rahab should remain standing."**

Play the game. Afterward say: **"The Israelites won this battle without drawing a sword, without attacking. All they did was follow God's instructions. They marched around the walls of Jericho. They then blew trumpets and yelled. That's all that needed to happen for the walls to fall. God kept God's promise. And the same happened with Rahab. Even though everything fell in the city and everyone died, Rahab didn't. She and everyone in her house were kept safe because of God's promise. We, too, can trust God to keep God's promises."**

Tongue Twisters

Scripture: Belshazzar (Daniel 5); Delilah (Judges 16); Hagar (Genesis 16); Methuselah (Genesis 5:25-27); Onesimus (Philemon); and Vashti (Esther 1–2)

This Game Teaches: The Bible isn't boring because there is always something new to discover in it.

Materials: None

• • • • • • • • • • • • • • • • •

80

Game: Have children sit in a circle. (Or if you have more than ten children present, form two teams with about the same number of players.) Say: **"We're going to play a game like the game of telephone. I'm going to whisper the name of a person from the Bible into the ear of one person. That person then whispers the word to the next person and so on. Now, you can only whisper the word once. If you aren't sure what you heard, just whisper what you think you heard. These names will sound strange, so just keep going. Then the last person to hear the word will say the word aloud to the group. Ready?"**

Each time, start with a different child so that the same child doesn't have to report the word to the group at the end of every game. Use names from the Bible, such as these:

- **Belshazzar** (Daniel 5 tells about how this guy took stuff from the church and used it for parties.)
- **Delilah** (Judges 16 tells of how she cut off Samson's hair to make him lose all his strength.)
- **Hagar** (Genesis 16 says that she was the mother of Ishmael.)
- **Methuselah** (Genesis 5:25-27 says that this man lived to be 969 years old.)
- **Onesimus** (Philemon tells the story of Onesimus being his slave.)
- **Vashti** (Esther 1-2 says Vashti was a beautiful queen who also had a lot of self-respect.)

Afterward say: **"Some people think the Bible is boring, but there are many interesting people in the Bible. Some have funny names. Some do weird things. That's why learning about the Bible can be so interesting."**

Three Claps

Scripture: The crucifixion and resurrection of Christ
(Matthew 27–28; Mark 15–16; Luke 23–24; John 18–20)

This Game Teaches: Several events happened from the time
Jesus was taken before Pilot until the Resurrection. The
story provides hints on how to live as Christians.

Materials: One flip chart and one marker for every five or
six children; one (or more) older child (a third- to sixth-
grader) for each group; Bibles

• • • • • • • • • • • • • • • • • •

Game: Form groups of five or six that include one older child
per group. Give each group a flip chart and marker.
Designate the older child as the recorder for the group.

Say: **"We're going to play a memory game. As a group, try
to name as many details as you can about the events that
happened from the time Jesus was taken before Pilot,
through the Crucifixion, and finally to the
Resurrection. The recorder will write the details on
the flip chart. Once three details are listed,
stand up as a group
and clap three
times. Then sit
down and
name more
details. When
three more
details are
listed, stand
up and clap
three times.
Keep doing
this until I
tell you to
stop.
"Why am I
asking you to clap**

81

three times? Because that's an important detail in the story. The number three appears many times. For example, it became dark for three hours during the Crucifixion. When Jesus called out to God, it was three o'clock. There were three people hanging on three crosses. And when Jesus rose from the dead, it was on the third day. Ready? Begin."

Do this without Bibles. If the children really struggle, however, consider giving each group a Bible to read the story aloud and identify details.

After the game ends, say: **"A lot happened from the time Jesus was taken before Pilot until Jesus rose from the dead. When we read stories in the Bible, not only is it important to understand the basic story, but it's also important to learn the details. These details give the story richness and provide hints on how to live as Christians."**

I See You

Scripture: Saul is made king, but he hides (1 Samuel 10:20-24)

This Game Teaches: Even though you may think you're hiding, you can be found.

Materials: A play area (either indoors or outside) with lots of hiding places; a sturdy chair

• • • • • • • • • • • • • • • • •

Game: Ask for a volunteer. Place the chair in the center of the play area. Say: **"We're going to play a game about Samuel looking for Saul. This child** (point to the volunteer) **is Samuel. Samuel is going to hide his eyes and count aloud to twenty. The rest of you are to hide. Now when Samuel gets to twenty, he'll stand on this chair. When he sees a child, he will call out the name of the child and the hiding place. If that is correct, the child must come out and join Samuel. Together the two of them can continue to look, but they cannot leave their position. We'll see how many children they can see from their spot."** Play the game. As children join Samuel, have them stand near, not on, the chair. Repeat the game again, if you wish, with a different Samuel.

82

Afterward say: **"Even though you may think you're hiding, you can be found. In this Bible story, the people can't find Saul. They want to make him king. But God knew where Saul was. God told the people that Saul was hiding in the baggage, and Saul was found."**

It's Getting Crowded

Scripture: Entering the ark (Genesis 7:7-9)

This Game Teaches: The ark was big and held a lot of people and animals, but everyone still needed to work together. It's good to work together.

Materials: A concrete play area (such as a sidewalk, patio, or parking lot); a warm day; chalk

• • • • • • • • • • • • • • • • •

83

Game: Begin by drawing a large square on the concrete with chalk. The square should easily hold all the children present.

Say: **"Noah built an ark. This is our ark. Let's all get inside."** Once the children are inside, have them step out again. Draw a smaller square inside the larger square, moving about six inches to one foot in from the larger square. Say: **"You know, when you put animals and people in an ark two by two, well, pretty soon, the space feels like it's getting smaller because of all the bodies. Now let's try to get inside this new ark."** Have children get inside the smaller box. Continue drawing smaller squares to make it more challenging for children. At some point, the older children may begin holding the smaller children. Encourage children to be creative in squeezing everyone in without hurting one another.

When the children finish the game, say: **"You were smart and sensitive in getting everyone to fit when the space became smaller. The ark was big and held lots of people and animals, but everyone had to work together. Thanks for working together so well."**

Arrested!

Scripture: The apostles are thrown into jail (Acts 5:17-26)
This Game Teaches: Miracles happen when you follow God.
Materials: A real or paper lock; a mock jail

• • • • • • • • • • • • • • • • •

Game: With the children's assistance, set up a mock jail (for example, place chairs together with the backs facing outward). Create a paper lock or put a real lock on the door of the mock jail (for example, hang a paper lock on the back of one of the chairs).

Create four groups. Have one group be the *guards*, one group be the *police*, one group be the *apostles*, and one group be the *Sadducees* (or priests). Say:

"Before we begin the game, let me briefly tell you this story. Then I want you to reenact it when I give you whispered clues. Ready? The Sadducees (or the priests) became very jealous of the apostles, who were the followers of Jesus. They decided to stop the apostles, so they had the police arrest them and put them in jail. Guards made sure they couldn't get out. The prison doors were locked. The Sadducees left. That night an angel came and helped the apostles get out of jail. They went back to preaching. In the morning, the Sadducees saw the apostles. They ran to the jail. The guards were still there and so were the locks!"

Have the children stand in position. Whisper these commands, pausing between them.

- The apostles are preaching. The Sadducees are whispering ideas of how to get rid of the apostles.
- The Sadducees ask the police to arrest the apostles.
- The apostles are arrested and thrown in jail.
- The guards make sure they don't escape.
- The angel comes and lets them out. (The leader or another child could be the angel.)
- The apostles preach again. The Sadducees see them.
- The Sadducees run to the jail. The guards are still there and so are the locked locks.

Repeat the game, having the groups change roles. Encourage the children to be lively and dramatic.

After the game ends, say: **"No one knows how the apostles got out of jail without the locks being touched. There are a lot of miracles in the Bible we don't understand. But what we can understand is this: Miracles happen when you follow God."**

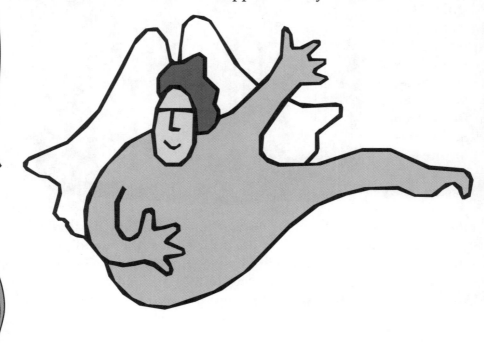

Wash and Eat

Scripture: Jesus washes the disciples' feet (John 13)
This Game Teaches: We need to serve others; no job is too unimportant for us to do.
Materials: A bowl of warm water; a towel; a bunch of grapes

• • • • • • • • • • • • • • • • •

Game: This game works well right before a snack break. Place the grapes on a table in the snack area. Have all the children take off their shoes and socks. Wash their feet one by one. Once children have had their feet washed and dried, they can go to the table and have a snack of grapes.

As you're washing children's feet, talk about the story of Jesus washing the disciples' feet. Include background information, such as that during the time when Jesus lived, when people entered a house their feet were washed to remove the dust. In the Bible, people wore sandals and walked on dusty roads. Their feet were dirty when they came to a house, and needed to be washed. Usually, a servant or the hired help washed people's feet—never the owner of the house. When Jesus washed the disciples' feet, he was teaching them the importance of serving others.

Afterward say: **"Although we don't have jobs such as washing people's feet when guests come to our house, there are still some jobs that we don't like. Jobs like taking out the garbage, changing the cat litter, cleaning the bathroom, or cleaning up our rooms. Jesus wants us to serve others. And there is no job that is too unimportant for us to do."**

85

Doing a Lot;
Doing Little

Scripture: The parable of the three servants and talents
(Matthew 25:14-30)
This Game Teaches: It's better to act and work with what we
have than to be afraid and do nothing.
Materials: Several pieces of 8½-x-11-inch paper; markers; two
balls; an empty can; sixteen pennies; a table with chairs

. . . .

Game: Form three groups with about the same number of
children in each group. Have one group sit around a table
with paper and markers and give that group five pennies to
put in the middle of the table. Encourage each child to draw a
picture. Have another group go to another area and play with
two balls, doing whatever they like to do for fun. Give them two
pennies for safekeeping. Have the third group go to another area
with an empty can. Give that group one penny to put into the can.
Have this group act lazy.

As the first group draws pictures, add five pennies to their pile.
As the second group plays with balls, add two pennies to their
pile. Do not give the third group anything. After a time, stop the
game. Have the first group show the pictures it drew to the rest of
the children. Have the second group demonstrate a game they
played with the balls. Ask children in the third group what they
did. Then ask each group to return the pennies to you.

After the game ends, say: **"Jesus tells the parable of giving
5,000 coins to one man, 2,000 coins to another man, and 1,000
coins to another man. The one with 5,000 coins used the money
to make a total of 10,000 coins. The one with 2,000 coins used
the money to make a total of 4,000 coins. The last one became
afraid and lazy and hid the coins by burying them. This parable
talks about how important it is to act—to do something with the
gifts we've been given. Maybe that's drawing pictures. Maybe
it's playing with balls. Maybe it's reading books. Whatever it is,
when we use what we have, God is happy."**

In the Dark

Scripture: God's covenant with Abram (Genesis 15)
This Game Teaches: God is with us—even when it's dark and we can't see God.
Materials: 8½-x-11-inch pieces of paper; two markers; two blindfolds

• • • • • • • • • • • • • • • • •

Game: Form two teams. Give each team several 8½-x-11-inch pieces of paper, a marker, and a blindfold.

Say: **"Choose one player from your team to start. Give that person a piece of paper and a marker. Blindfold the person. In a moment, I will whisper something to draw in the ear of the blindfolded child. He or she must draw the object without trying to peek through the blindfold. The rest of you help the child stay on the paper. Do this quietly because after you finish, the other team will guess what the object is from the drawing."**

You may also want to darken the room to make the game more challenging. Whisper to the blindfolded child of one team to draw a *cow*. Whisper to the blindfolded child of the other team to draw a *goat*. After the children finish, take off the blindfolds (and turn on the lights if the room has been darkened). Have teams take turns guessing what the object is until one team correctly identifies the object. If teams struggle to do so after five tries, let the child tell what he or she drew.

Repeat the game but with a different child from each team being blindfolded. Continue to play the game a number of times. Use these objects as items for children to draw:

- One team draws a ram; the other team draws a dove.
- One team draws a smoking firepot; the other team draws a flaming torch.

After the game ends, say: **"In Genesis 15, God makes a covenant with Abram. This happened in the dark. The objects you drew were all part of the covenant. God is with us—even when it's dark and we can't see God."**

Giant Fall

Scripture: David and Goliath (1 Samuel 17)
This Game Teaches: Faithfulness wins out—not size.
Materials A large bag of rubber bands; an 8½-x-11-inch piece
of paper; masking tape; marker

• • • • • • • • • • • • • • • • • •

88

Game: With the marker, write "Goliath" in large letters on
an 8½-x-11-inch sheet of paper, and hang it on a wall about
eight feet from the floor. Clear the nearby area.

Have children stand about six to ten feet away from the
piece of paper. Give each person several rubber bands. Say:
**"We're going to play a game about David and Goliath. These
rubber bands are slingshots. You're David. That's Goliath** (point
to the piece of paper). **When I tell you to begin, start aiming for
Goliath with your rubber bands. As soon as you release your
rubber band, grab another and aim again."** Establish ground
rules, such as only aiming at the Goliath paper and not aiming at
people. Make sure children are not in each other's way to avoid
accidents. Then begin the game.

After the game ends, say:
**"Most people like this
story because it
shows how the big
and the strong
don't always
win, even
though they
usually can. In
this story, it was
faithfulness that
won out—not
size, not strength.
David won
because he
remained faithful
to God."**

You Can Walk!

Scripture: The healing of the man at the pool (John 5:1-9)
This Game Teaches: Jesus helped others, just as we should help others.
Materials: None

• • • • • • • • • • • • • • • • • •

Game: Ask for a volunteer. Have that person be Jesus. Say: **"The rest of you are going to be the people who have come to the pool to be healed. Either lie on the ground, sit, crawl, or walk hunched over with a pretend cane. Then Jesus will come around. When he or she touches you and says, 'Walk,' straighten up and begin to walk. Once you've been healed, help Jesus touch others in the room until everyone is healed."**

Play the game.
Afterward say: **"The man in John 5 had been unable to walk for thirty-eight years. Most likely he had given up all hope. But Jesus came for all people—those who had hope and those who didn't. He helped others, just as we can help others. Although we may not have the gift of healing, we all have the ability to help someone in some way."**

Are We There Yet?

Scripture: After the Israelites wander in the desert for forty years, Joshua leads them into the Promised Land (Joshua 3:14-17)

This Game Teaches: It's important to stick with the journey and not always focus on where we want to end up.

Materials: Decide what areas you want to visit with the children (such as a certain number of rooms or areas outside).

• • • • • • • • • • • • • • • •

Game: Briefly tell the story about the Israelites wandering in the desert for forty years. Say: **"Now, we're going to pretend we're the Israelites. Line up behind me and follow me. Let's start wandering through the desert. Repeat whatever I say and do."**

90

Create an interesting journey by weaving in and out and doing different actions. (If lots of older children are in your group, have them take turns leading the group.) Some possible ideas to try are:

- It's a hot day. There's not much water. We're dragging. We're thirsty.
- We're walking in circles.
- Shhh! There's a snake. Let's tiptoe and not bother it.
- It's getting rocky. (Slowly step on and over a chair here and there to keep everyone safe.)
- It's night. Let's get some sleep.
- It's morning. Another day to stretch, get up, and start walking again.
- Time to stop and cook a meal.
- Let's eat the meal.
- Let's clean up the dishes.
- Let's get back to walking.
- Uh-oh! There's danger behind us. Quick! Let's run!

- This is getting boring. Let's dance.
- Time to get back on the road. Let's get back to walking.
- There it is! (Point.) There's the Promised Land.
- We have to cross a river.
- We made it. We're at the Promised Land! Let's cheer.

After the game ends, say: **"Forty years is a long time to wander in the desert. I bet people wanted to give up at times. Sometimes, we feel that way, too. Maybe we're trying to learn how to play the piano or how to play soccer. It sometimes seems as if we'll never get there. But when we stick with it, we will get there. It may take us a long time, but the important thing is to keep on going, keep on following, keep on practicing—just like the Israelites."**

Alone and Together

Scripture: Jesus sends out the disciples (Mark 6:6*b*-13)
This Game Teaches: Sometimes we work with other Christians; sometimes we work alone.
Materials: None

• • • • • • • • • • • • • • • • •

91

Game: Say: **"We're going to play a game. Every time I name a motion, do that action twice. When I use the word 'I,' do the motion by yourself. When I use the word 'we,' come together as a large group and do the motion together twice."**

Name motions, such as these:

• I can talk.
• We can talk.
• I can eat.
• We can eat.
• I can say hello.
• We can say hello.
• I can hug.
• We can hug.
• I can dance.
• We can dance.

After the game, say: **"Jesus sent the disciples out to help others. Sometimes they did these things alone. Sometimes they did things in groups. As Christians, sometimes we work with other Christians; sometimes we work alone. Both ways are good."**

Ten Yucky Things

Scripture: The ten plagues (Exodus 7–12)
This Game Teaches: The plagues made life miserable for the Egyptians. It's good for people to listen to God.
Materials: A place where the lights can easily be turned off

• • • • • • • • • • • • • • • • • •

Game: Say: **"We're going to play a game about the ten plagues. Before we begin, let's go through the actions of the ten plagues."**

Lead the group in acting out the plagues:

92

- Plague #1—*Blood* (Say: **"The river is bloody! Ooo! Yuck!"**)
- Plague #2—*Frogs* (Hop like a frog.)
- Plague #3—*Gnats* (Swat at imaginary mosquitoes.)
- Plague #4—*Flies* (Buzz!)
- Plague #5—*Death of animals* (Lie on the ground and close your eyes.)
- Plague #6—*Boils* (Scratch imaginary sores on your body.)
- Plague #7—*Hail* (Squat down and cover your head.)
- Plague #8—*Locusts* (Jump like a grasshopper.)
- Plague #9—*Darkness* (Turn off the light.)
- Plague #10—*Death of the firstborn* (Everyone cry.)

Call out the number of the plague and the name of the plague. For example, call out plague number three and say: **"gnats!"** Have children do the activity of swatting at imaginary mosquitoes.

Play the game once by calling out the plagues in chronological order. You may need to remind children what actions they do with each plague the first time through. Then play again by mixing up the numbers, calling out some numbers closer together so children have to move more quickly.

After the game is finished, say: **"For us, the ten plagues sound rather interesting and funny. But they weren't funny to the Egyptians. In fact, these ten plagues made their lives horrible. The Egyptians wouldn't have had to go through these ten plagues if they had listened to Moses and let the Israelites go, as God had commanded. It's good for us to listen to God."**

Clean and Repair

Scripture: Repairing the temple and finding the scroll
(2 Kings 22–23)

This Game Teaches: We need to care for what we have.

Materials: A small cleaning or repair project at the church
that children can do (such as putting away toys in a nurs-
ery, picking up litter on the church grounds, refilling and
straightening literature racks in the church narthex); a
rolled-up piece of paper that includes the words "God
likes it when we help" with a rubber band around it

• • • • • • • • • • • • • • • • • •

93

Game: Hide the scroll in the area in which you will work.
Say: **"In 2 Kings 22, Josiah was the king. As incredible as it
sounds, he became a king when he was only eight years
old. He saw that God's house needed some help, so he
asked the people to clean and repair it. That's what we're
going to do now—clean and repair our church."**

Do the project. Hope that one of the children will find the scroll.
If one does, don't let it be opened until the project is finished. If
no one notices the scroll, point it out at the end of your activity.
Have an older child read it aloud.

Afterward say: **"When the people were repairing God's house
in 2 Kings, a scroll was also
found. It, too, had words
about how God wanted
God's people to act. We need
to care for what we have.
That includes our church,
our bodies, our friends,
our families, and all people. God likes it when we
help."**

Body Parts

Scripture: Christ is like a body, which has many parts (1 Corinthians 12:12-31)

This Game Teaches: Every body part of every person is essential.

Materials: An index card for each child; markers; masking tape

· · · · · · · · · · · · · · · · · ·

Game: Make an index card for each child. For example, if five children are present, on five different cards write the following: *foot, hand, eye, leg,* and *arm*. (Draw pictures of these body parts if you have children present who haven't mastered reading yet.) Then give each child a card. For six to ten children, make duplicates of the *foot, hand, ear,* and *eye* cards. (Make as many duplicates as you have children.) If eleven children are present, make the original five cards listed above, along with these additional cards: *neck, arm, leg, torso, mouth,* and *nose*. In groups of more than eleven children, make duplicate cards of the body parts that people have two of, such as: *foot, hand, eye, leg,* and *arm*. Give an index card to each child. Have all of them tape the cards to the front of their shirts with masking tape.

Say: **"We're going to play a**

94

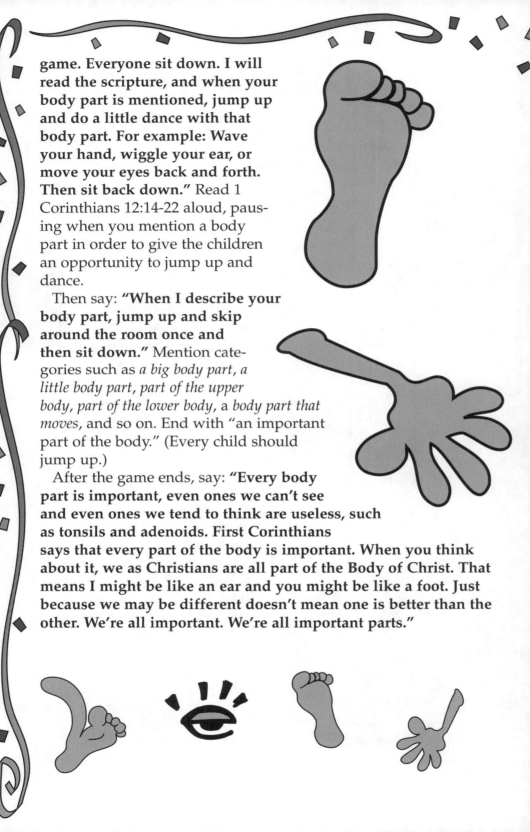

game. Everyone sit down. I will read the scripture, and when your body part is mentioned, jump up and do a little dance with that body part. For example: Wave your hand, wiggle your ear, or move your eyes back and forth. Then sit back down." Read 1 Corinthians 12:14-22 aloud, pausing when you mention a body part in order to give the children an opportunity to jump up and dance.

Then say: "When I describe your body part, jump up and skip around the room once and then sit down." Mention categories such as *a big body part*, *a little body part*, *part of the upper body*, *part of the lower body*, a *body part that moves*, and so on. End with "an important part of the body." (Every child should jump up.)

After the game ends, say: "Every body part is important, even ones we can't see and even ones we tend to think are useless, such as tonsils and adenoids. First Corinthians says that every part of the body is important. When you think about it, we as Christians are all part of the Body of Christ. That means I might be like an ear and you might be like a foot. Just because we may be different doesn't mean one is better than the other. We're all important. We're all important parts."

New Creations

Scripture: God creates animals (Genesis 1:20-25)

This Game Teaches: We have a creative God who gave us the gift of creativity, too.

Materials: A palm-sized ball of clay or play dough for each child

• • • • • • • • • • • • • • • • •

Game: Give each child some clay. Say: **"In Genesis 1:20-25, on the fifth and sixth days, God created animals. Animals of the sky. Animals of the water. Animals of the land. Now I want you to pretend you're God. Create your own animal—an animal that has never been on earth before. As you create your animal think of a name and where it lives (such as on land, in the water, or in the sky)."**

When the children finish, have each person show her or his animal creation to the group. In addition, have the child lead the group in making the sound of their animal and demonstrate the way it moves.

Afterward say: **"Our God is a creative God. God made all kinds of amazing animals, plants, and places. God also made each one of us. And God gave each of us an imagination and the gift of creativity."**

95

A Gentle Carry

Scripture: Saul's followers help him escape by lowering him in a basket (Acts 9:20-25)

This Game Teaches: We can be clever and work together to help others.

Materials: An unfitted sheet from a twin or full-size bed

• • • • • • • • • • • • • • • • •

96

Game: Ask a volunteer to lie down in the middle of an unfitted sheet. Have the rest of the group circle around the sheet and grab the edges. Together have the group slightly roll up the edges of the sheet and get a firm grip. Have the group lift and carry the child across the room and then gently set her or him down. Ask for another volunteer to be carried in the sheet. Do this as many as times as children would like.

After the game, say: **"After Saul was converted, he began preaching about Jesus being the Son of God. Some loved to hear this, but others wanted to kill Saul. So Saul's followers decided to help him, and late one night they put him in a large basket. Then they lowered him through an opening in the wall of the city so he could escape. We can be clever and work together to help others, just as Saul's followers did."**

Manna, Manna, Everywhere!

Scripture: Manna appears on the ground for people to eat (Numbers 11:4-9)

This Game Teaches: The Israelites grew weary of eating manna again and again. Instead of complaining, we can look for ways to make something boring more interesting.

Materials: A bag of cotton balls and a container (such as a bucket, box, or basket)

• • • • • • • • • • • • • • • • •

Game: Place the container at one end of the play area and have the children gather around as you hold the bag of cotton balls at least three feet away from the container.

Say: **"We're going to play a game about manna. These cotton balls are going to be the manna. When they fall on the ground, pick one or two up—no more than two—and take them to the container. Drop them in before running back to pick up one or two more. The game ends when all the manna is in the bucket."**

Throw the cotton balls out with great force in all four directions so they don't all glob together. After the children finish the first game, play it two more times. Then ask: **"When was the game most fun? When was it least fun? Why?"** Next say: **"At first the Israelites were thrilled to get manna from heaven. They were hungry because they didn't have food. But after a while, they got tired of eating manna over and over again. That happens to us, too. It's exciting to get something new, like a new game. But after a while, it often becomes boring. If they tried, the Israelites could have found ways to make manna interesting, just as we can make the same old things interesting by adding a new spin or twist to them."**

Follow Me

Scripture: Jesus calls the four fishermen (Mark 1:14-18)
This Game Teaches: Following Jesus looks easier than it is.
Materials: A long playing area; masking tape; three rolls of
toilet paper

. . . .

98

Game: Form three groups and designate a leader for each
group. Have children line up single-file, with the lines about
two feet apart. Mark each group's starting line with a piece of
masking tape on the floor. About ten feet in front of each
group, mark a finish line with masking tape. Give each group
a roll of toilet paper, and have them unroll it slightly so that the
end can be taped to the floor at the starting line. Tell groups to be
careful not to break the toilet paper.

Say: **"The leader of your group is Jesus. When I say to begin,
Jesus will say, 'Follow me' and lead the group toward the finish
line** (point to the finish line). **The rest of you will take turns
unrolling the toilet paper from the starting line to the finish
line. Each person will unroll the toilet paper for five steps
before the next person in line unrolls it for five steps. The goal
is not to do this quickly, but to do this without ripping the toilet
paper. If the toilet paper rips, even slightly, you
have to go back to the beginning and start
again."**

Begin the game. After the game
ends, say: **"Following Jesus looks
easy, but actually it is not.
There are bumps along the
way. We lose our concentra-
tion. We get distracted. We
get busy. But if we're careful,
and think about what we're
doing by learning as much as
we can about what it means to
be a Christian, we can become
better followers of Jesus."**

The Fiery Furnace

Scripture: Shadrach, Meshach, and Abednego in the furnace (Daniel 3:19-30)

This Game Teaches: We should follow what we believe God wants us to do.

Materials: Access to the boiler or furnace room of your church; permission to use the room and information about what not to touch; another adult supervisor

• • • • • • • • • • • • • • • • •

99

Game: Tell the story of Daniel 3. Take the class near the furnace or boiler room, which will be behind closed doors. Ask for four volunteers: one to be the guard who opens the furnace door, and the other three to be Shadrach, Meshach, and Abednego, who get thrown into the furnace. Have the other adult stay out of sight in the furnace room until the three children have entered. (That adult will supervise the children and also act as the angel who appeared.) Shut the door and reenact the story.

The guard will open the door, gently push the three children inside toward the furnace, and then pretend to die from the heat. The adult posted inside the furnace room should step into view and encourage the three children to walk and dance around. Briefly talk about how King Nebuchadnezzar couldn't believe his eyes. Not only were Shadrach, Meshach, and Abednego walking around, but there was a fourth person with them—an angel who protected them.

Invite everyone out of the furnace. Then have the entire class step inside for a brief moment to feel, smell, hear, and see what it's like to be in a furnace or boiler room.

Afterward say: **"King Nebuchadnezzar was angry that these three men obeyed God instead of the king. That's why he threw them into the furnace. But God protected them from harm. We, too, should follow what we believe God wants us to do."**

Money, Money, Money

Scripture: Samuel's greedy sons (1 Samuel 8)
This Game Teaches: Giving is more fun than greediness.
Materials: Ten to twenty pennies for each child

• • • • • • • • • • • • • • • • • •

100

Game: Form groups of three or four. Give each child ten to twenty pennies. Say: **"We're going to play this game twice. The first time, work as hard as you can to guard your pennies while also trying to get as many pennies from the children in your group. The goal is to get as many pennies as you can. Any questions? Let's begin."**

Play the game. After a couple of minutes, stop the game. Ask: **"How did you feel as you played this game? Why?"** Then say: **"Let's play this game another way. This time, try to give away all your pennies. If anyone gives you any pennies, give those away, too. The goal is to end up with no pennies. Any questions? Let's begin."**

Play the game. After a couple of minutes, stop the game. Ask: **"How did you feel as you played this game? Why? Which game did you like better? Why?"**

After the game say: **"Samuel had sons who were greedy. They tried to take away everybody's pennies and wouldn't share any that they owned. Although it's fun to have money, it's also fun to give to others."**

Shhh! Zechariah

Scripture: Gabriel foretells the birth of John the Baptist (Luke 1:5-25)

This Game Teaches: Our voices are an important part of ourselves. When Zechariah didn't believe the angel, he lost his voice until his baby was born. It's important to believe messages from God, even if they seem impossible.

Materials: None

• • • • • • • • • • • • • • • • •

Game: Ask for a volunteer to be the angel Gabriel. (If you have young children playing, choose a child age eight or older to be the angel.) Say: **"We're going to play a type of Bible tag. This child is Gabriel, and Gabriel is it** (point to the volunteer). **The rest of you are Zechariah. As you walk around the room, sing your favorite song and try to keep from being tagged. Once you are tagged, continue to walk around the room, but you must become silent. The activity will end when the room is completely quiet. Ready? Start singing and moving."**

Give Gabriel time to move around the room, tagging children to make them stop singing. The continuing motion will make it more challenging for Gabriel to find everyone to tag, since he or she will need to listen carefully to figure out whom to tag. (If your group is made up mainly of younger children, have the tagged children stop singing and stop moving to make the activity easier.) After the game ends, say: **"Gabriel came to tell Zechariah that a baby was going to be born to his wife, Elizabeth. Since both Elizabeth and Zechariah were very old, Zechariah didn't believe Gabriel. When Gabriel left, Zechariah realized he could no longer speak. He lost his voice until the baby, John the Baptist, was born. It's important to believe the important messages from God—even if they seem impossible."**

Appendix

GAMES AND TOUGH TOPICS

Some children say the Bible and Christian education are boring. Television and computer games are more interesting to them. They get tired of sitting still, acting polite, and hearing Bible stories that don't have much sense of drama to them. So when they don't feel stimulated, some draw armored tanks on the backs of their student booklets, while others sometimes start a rubber-band fight when you turn your back.

Yet the Bible is rich with drama. Where else can you find a story about a man who needs his long hair in order to be strong enough to push over temples? Where else can you see the staff of Aaron become a snake when it's thrown to the ground? Where else can you see a sea opening up and letting the good guys through before closing up to drown all the bad guys? The Bible is full of fascinating stories.

In fact, the Bible sometimes can seem more graphic than the evening news. Noah got drunk and lay naked where others could see him. David murdered and committed adultery. Judas committed suicide. Stephen was stoned. And throughout the Old Testament, the Israelites engaged in all kinds of gruesome battles. What do we do with the stories that make us uncomfortable as adults?

We can address certain stories and leave out eye-raising details that children don't need to know. For example, the game "Hide and Sneak" (game 69) is based on Joshua 2 where Rahab the prostitute helps a couple of the Israelites escape. Rahab's profession is

140

never mentioned. It's not important for the game—or the teaching point. However, the story is rarely addressed at all with young children. It's almost as if we think that children will somehow pick up the edited-out details by osmosis.

But children won't. Children are interested in drama, and as you begin to expose children to the biblical drama, many will become more interested in Christian education. Boys, in particular, love all the wars and battles in the Bible. Sometimes I play games based on these battles, although I'm very clear about the point of the story and the game, and it's never about the battle itself. I, like many people in church, emphasize peace-and-justice issues, since I do not want children to act in aggressive ways. Children must learn appropriate ways to act and interact with others. However, sometimes we stifle their energy and their imaginations by placing too many constraints on them.

Unfortunately, children will act aggressively at times whether we play war games with them or not. "We all have feelings of anger and aggression," says the American Academy of Pediatrics. "These impulses are normal and healthy."[1] That applies not only to children but also to adults. In addition, research conducted by the Gesell Institute of Human Development revealed that 70 percent of five-year-old girls and 65 percent of five-year-old boys told stories with violence as the main theme. Violence included anything from aggression to accidents to people getting hurt.[2]

Although it's true we want children to talk about their feelings and not act aggressively, we also don't want them to lock away all their energy. This sometimes results in children becoming aggressive just because they've been siting too long and have become frustrated and irritated about not being able to move.

So how do you handle this issue?

- **State acceptable and unacceptable behavior**—Be clear that you will not tolerate biting, hitting, bullying, temper tantrums, demanding behavior, or destruction. Explain what children can expect when these behaviors occur and tell their parents, too. Know that you should—and can—expect more out of a ten-year-old than a three-year-old, but that you want *all* children to act in caring ways toward themselves and others.

- **Be firm and consistent in addressing inappropriate behavior**—Stating boundaries is one thing, but enforcing them is another. If you want children to take you seriously, you need to take seriously every inappropriate behavior that arises. Address it immediately and firmly.

- **Clarify your views of imaginary play**—Although most churches won't allow children to bring play guns and other weapons to church, children will still turn other objects into items for war. Pencils become guns or swords. Take-home lessons get folded into stealth fighters. Children make noises that sound like explosions and dropping bombs. When these events start to happen, I pull out a game to get the children's energy flowing in another direction.

- **Tap into children's curiosity in appropriate ways**—A few of the games in this book address some of the uncomfortable stories of the Bible. "The Israelites: The Winners" (game 60), for fourth- to sixth-graders, is based on the story of the Israelites going to war against the Midianites. "Arrested!" (game 84), for mixed ages, is about the apostles being thrown into jail. "Giant Fall" (game 88) is a reenactment of David and Goliath where children aim rubber bands at a mock Goliath. Although your church may decide these games are inappropriate and not use them, I've found they enhance rather than contradict the teaching of peace and justice. For example, in "Giant Fall," I purposely use the word "aim" but never the word "shoot." I also intentionally use the *word* "Goliath" instead of a *picture* of Goliath to reinforce the notion that we don't aim things at people's faces.[3] Although these may seem like trivial differences, I've found them helpful in allowing children to act like children while also setting boundaries on aggressive behavior.

- **Know your children**—Some children seem to be inherently more aggressive than others. Sometimes a child in your group hasn't been taught how to control aggressive tendencies. Whenever I have a child or a couple of children who struggle with controlling their impulses, I am much choosier about the games that I play with them. I will not play games such as "The Israelites: The Winners," "Arrested!" or "Giant Fall," but focus instead on games that help children cooperate and work together, such as "Two! Two! Two!" (game 4), "Caring Cornelius" (game 44), "Building the Tower of Babel" (game 62), and "Are We There Yet?" (game 90).

- **Focus on the fun**—It's easy to get caught up in the problems of a particular child who acts up often. When this happens, we unintentionally create a climate that's more tense. No group of children is ever completely quiet and cooperative. Be firm about behavior but also allow children to be children. Have fun with them. Make these games enjoyable. And everyone—you and the children—will have a good time.

Creating Your Own Games

When I first began creating and adapting games, I'd start with a familiar game and change it slightly. Terry Orlick in his book *The Cooperative Sports & Games Book: Challenge Without Competition* shows how to play cooperative musical chairs with preschoolers. It is a game based on the old standby, musical chairs, but with a new twist. Chairs are removed, children are not, and all the children have to sit on the remaining chair.[4] In fact, many of the games in this book are either adaptations of familiar games or a new game that has an element from one game and maybe an element from another. Creating games from scratch happens rarely, and when they do pop up, only a few are memorable, like the game "Knots."[5]

Children are the ones who taught me the most about adapting and creating new games. When I started teaching, I prepared lessons by doing what was prepared and written in the denominational curriculum our church was using. Rarely did I stray from what was suggested. It wasn't until some of the children started getting bored and restless, since many denominational curriculums don't include physical games, that I began asking them for ideas. At first, they wanted to play some games, which we did. After we did that for a while, they began to get bored with the standard games. Suddenly, "Duck Duck, Gray Duck" became "Duck, Duck, Joke Duck" where the child tagged had to jump up and say a joke as quickly as possible before running. (I didn't think of this game, one of my students did.) Soon all the children were clamoring with ideas. "How about 'Duck, Duck, Sing-a-Song Duck'? or 'Duck, Duck, Somersault Duck'?" The crazier or more unusual, the better. Then we'd try it. Some worked; some flopped. But we always had a lot of fun—and we still do.

Now, however, I take a different approach to creating games. I start with stories from scripture. I read a specific story, such as Samson and Delilah in Judges 16, and I look for the literal movement in the story. Since the story centers around Samson's hair, I began wondering what I could do with that. When I looked in an illustrated children's Bible and saw Samson's long hair, I began to think of a wig. Soon the game "Haircut Horror" (game 71), emerged.

Like anything you create, you'll find yourself in trial-and-error mode a lot of the time. Often the games I thought would go over well didn't go over at all. Sometimes the best games that developed were ones where the children didn't understand the instructions and played the game the way they thought they had heard it (which was new to me). In creating or adapting games, try these ideas:

• **Come up with as many ideas as possible**—Rarely does your first idea work. Sometimes I have four or five versions of one game until the final game takes form. Develop as many ideas as you can, and the more you can stretch yourself to produce ideas that don't seem realistic, the better.

- **Try new angles**—"Originality is one of the hallmarks of creative thinking," writes Mihaly Csikszentmihalyi in *Creativity: Flow and the Psychology of Discovery and Invention*.[6] Creative people are ordinary people who see a new twist or new angle. What happens if you change one word of a game title? What if you play a game backward? What if you have to play a game in silence? What if you adjust the game's speed? What if all players have to have a partner for the game? What if? What if? What if? These are the questions to ask to find new angles.

- **Take a risk**—A creative new game often flies in the face of convention. A new game is risky. You'll meet up with skeptics ("that will never work"), the lazy ("do we have to do that?"), and the self-conscious ("you want me to do *that*?"). That's why it's important to participate with children, especially if the game has a bit of foolishness to it. Even if a game fails, that's a good learning experience for you—and the children. Modeling how to deal with things that don't work or go as planned is an important skill that children usually learn by adults *telling* them about it rather than *showing* them. In addition, what child wouldn't clap and smile when you create a game that works really well and you kick your heels in the air afterward?

Notes

1. Steven P. Shelov, M.D., editor in chief, American Academy of Pediatrics, *Caring for Your Baby and Young Child: Birth to Age 5* (New York: Bantam, 1991), 507.
2. Louise Bates Ames, Ph.D., and Frances L. Ilg, M.D., *Your Five-Year-Old: Sunny and Serene* (New York: Dell, 1979), 38-39.
3. Children will aim at a "word" not at a "picture" so they are aiming at a concept, rather than a person's face. A picture of Goliath may make a child think he or she can aim at people.
4. Terry Orlick, *The Cooperative Sports & Games Book: Challenge Without Competition* (New York: Pantheon, 1978), 64-65.
5. For instructions on how to play the game "Knots," see: *The New Games Book*, edited by Andrew Fluegelman (New York: Dolphin, 1976), 69.
6. Mihaly Csikszentmihalyi, *Creativity: Flow and the Psychology of Discovery and Invention* (New York: HarperPerennial, 1996), 369.

Scripture Index